THE PREHISTORIC EARTH

THE AGE
OF MAMMALS

THE OLIGOCENE &
MIOCENE EPOCHS

THE PREHISTORIC EARTH

THE PREHISTORIC EARTH

THE AGE OF MAMMALS

THE OLIGOCENE & MIOCENE EPOCHS

Thom Holmes

CHELSEA HOUSE
PUBLISHERS
An imprint of Infobase Publishing

THE PREHISTORIC EARTH: The Age of Mammals

Chelsea House
An imprint of Infobase Publishing
132 West 31st Street
New York NY 10001

Library of Congress Cataloging-in-Publication Data

Holmes, Thom.
  The age of mammals : the Oligocene and Miocene epochs / Thom Holmes.
     p. cm. — (The prehistoric Earth)
  Includes bibliographical references and index.
  ISBN 978-0-8160-5964-5 (hardcover)
  1. Mammals, Fossil. 2. Paleontology—Oligocene. 3. Paleontology—Miocene. I. Title.
  QE881.H749 2009
  569—dc22   2008038329

Text design by Kerry Casey
Cover design by Salvatore Luongo
Section opener images © John Sibbick

Printed in the United States of America

Bang NMSG 10 9 8 7 6 5 4 3 2 1

This book is printed on acid-free paper.

CONTENTS

PREFACE

To be curious about the future one must know something about the past.

Humans have been recording events in the world around them for about 5,300 years. That is how long it has been since the Sumerian people, in a land that is today part of southern Iraq, invented the first known written language. Writing allowed people to document what they saw happening around them. The written word gave a new permanency to life. Language, and writing in particular, made history possible.

History is a marvelous human invention, but how do people know about things that happened before language existed? Or before humans existed? Events that took place before human record keeping began are called *prehistory*. Prehistoric life is, by its definition, any life that existed before human beings existed and were able to record for posterity what was happening in the world around them.

Prehistory is as much a product of the human mind as history. Scientists who specialize in unraveling clues of prehistoric life are called *paleontologists*. They study life that existed before human history, often hundreds of thousands and millions, and even billions, of years in the past. Their primary clues come from fossils of animals, plants, and other organisms, as well as geologic evidence about Earth's topography and climate. Through the skilled and often clever interpretation of fossils, paleontologists are able to reconstruct the appearances, lifestyles, environments, and relationships of ancient life-forms. While paleontology is grounded in a study of prehistoric life, it draws on many other sciences to complete an accurate picture of the past. Information from the fields of biology, zoology, geology, chemistry, meteorology, and even astrophysics is called into play to help the paleontologist view the past through the lens of today's knowledge.

If a writer were to write a history of all sports, would it be enough to write only about table tennis? Certainly not. On the shelves of bookstores and libraries, however, we find just such a slanted perspective toward the story of the dinosaurs. Dinosaurs have captured our imagination at the expense of many other equally fascinating, terrifying, and unusual creatures. Dinosaurs were not alone in the pantheon of prehistoric life, but it is rare to find a book that also mentions the many other kinds of life that came before and after the dinosaurs.

The Prehistoric Earth is a series that explores the evolution of life from its earliest forms 3.5 billion years ago until the emergence of modern humans about 300,000 years ago. Three volumes in the series trace the story of the dinosaurs. Seven other volumes are devoted to the kinds of animals that evolved before, during, and after the reign of the dinosaurs. *The Prehistoric Earth* covers the early explosion of life in the oceans; the invasion of the land by the first land animals; the rise of fishes, amphibians, reptiles, mammals, and birds; and the emergence of modern humans.

The Prehistoric Earth series is written for readers in middle school and high school. Based on the latest scientific findings in paleontology, *The Prehistoric Earth* is the most comprehensive and up-to-date series of its kind for this age group.

The first volume in the series, *Early Life*, offers foundational information about geologic time, Earth science, fossils, the classification of organisms, and evolution. This volume also begins the chronological exploration of fossil life that explodes with the incredible life-forms of the Precambrian and Cambrian Periods, more than 500 million years ago.

The remaining nine volumes in the series can be read chronologically. Each volume covers a specific geologic time period and describes the major forms of life that lived at that time. The books also trace the geologic forces and climate changes that affected the evolution of life through the ages. Readers of *The Prehistoric Earth* will see the whole picture of prehistoric life take shape. They will learn about forces that affect life on Earth, the directions that life can sometimes take, and ways in which all life-forms depend on each other in the environment. Along the way, readers also will meet many of the scientists who have made remarkable discoveries about the prehistoric Earth.

The language of science is used throughout this series, with ample definition and with an extensive glossary provided in each volume. Important concepts involving geology, evolution, and the lives of early animals are presented logically, step by step. Illustrations, photographs, tables, and maps reinforce and enhance the books' presentation of the story of prehistoric life.

While telling the story of prehistoric life, the author hopes that many readers will be sufficiently intrigued to continue studies on their own. For this purpose, throughout each volume, special "Think About It" sidebars offer additional insights or interesting exercises for readers who wish to explore certain topics. Each book in the series also provides a chapter-by-chapter bibliography of books, journals, and Web sites.

Only about one-tenth of 1 percent of all species of prehistoric animals are known from fossils. A multitude of discoveries remain to be made in the field of paleontology. It is with earnest, best wishes that I hope that some of these discoveries will be made by readers inspired by this series.

—Thom Holmes
Jersey City, New Jersey

ACKNOWLEDGMENTS

I want to thank the many dedicated and hardworking people at Chelsea House and Facts on File, some of whom I know but many of whom work behind the scenes. A special debt of gratitude goes to my editors—Frank Darmstadt, Brian Belval, Justine Ciovacco, Lisa Rand, and Shirley White—for their support and guidance in conceiving and making *The Prehistoric Earth* a reality. Frank and Brian were instrumental in fine-tuning the features of the series as well as accepting my ambitious plan for creating a comprehensive reference for students. Brian greatly influenced input during production. Shirley's excellent questions about the science behind the books contributed greatly to the readability of the result. The excellent copyediting of Mary Ellen Kelly was both thoughtful and vital to shaping the final manuscript. I thank Mary Ellen for her patience as well as her valuable review and suggestions that help make the book a success.

I am privileged to have worked with some of the brightest minds in paleontology on this series. Grégoire Métais of the Muséum National d'Histoire Naturelle in Paris reviewed the draft of *The Age of Mammals* and made many important suggestions that affected the course of the work. Grégoire also wrote the Foreword for the volume.

Breathing life into prehistoric creatures is also the work of natural history artists, many of whom have contributed to this series. I especially want to thank John Sibbick, a major contributor to the artwork seen in *The Prehistoric Earth*. John's work is renowned among paleontologists, many of whom he has worked with side by side.

In many ways, a set of books such as this requires years of preparation. Some of the work is educational, and I owe much gratitude to

Dr. Peter Dodson of the University of Pennsylvania for his gracious and inspiring tutelage over the years. I also thank Dr. William B. Gallagher of the New Jersey State Museum for lessons learned both in the classroom and in the historic fossil beds of New Jersey. Another dimension of preparation requires experience digging fossils, and for giving me these opportunities I thank my friends and colleagues who have taken me into the field with them, including Phil Currie, Rodolfo Coria, Matthew Lammana, Josh Smith, and Ruben Martinez.

Finally comes the work needed to put thoughts down on paper and complete the draft of a book, a process that always takes many more hours than I plan on. I thank Anne for bearing with my constant state of busy-ness, jokes about jawless fishes, and penguin notes, and for helping me remember the important things in life. You are an inspiration to me. I also thank my daughter, Shaina, the genius in the family and another constant inspiration, for always being supportive and humoring her dad's obsession with prehistoric life, even as he becomes part of it.

FOREWORD

Mammals are taxonomically and ecologically diverse vertebrates that burrow, fly, and swim, occupying a vast range of habitat via an amazing array of body shapes and sizes. Much of this relatively well-documented diversity evolved in the Cenozoic "Age of Mammals."

In his up-to-date overview of the Age of Mammals, Thom Holmes provides fascinating insights into the rise of mammals during the Paleocene Epoch (*The Rise of Mammals*), and the radiation of most of the extant groups of mammals that took place from the base of the Eocene up to Pleistocene Epochs (*The Age of Mammals*).

In fact, the early mammals originated and diversified in the Late Triassic to Early Jurassic (about 200 million years ago), during a major interval of ecological and environmental change, and therefore the Cenozoic represents only one-third of the evolutionary history of mammals. Although our knowledge about Mesozoic mammals is constantly growing, the evolutionary patterns drawn for the radiation of Cenozoic mammals is relatively well documented. It appears that the evolutionary history of Cenozoic mammals articulated around three major climatic events: the Paleocene-Eocene Thermal Maximum (about 55 million years ago); the Eocene-Oligocene transition, which is marked by a global cooling; and the successive glaciations that took place during the Pleistocene (about 1.8 million years ago to the present). This book not only provides an extensive and detailed review of extinct and living groups of mammals, but it also shows how the abiotic events (climate, geography) contributed to shaping the extant picture of mammal diversity and biogeography.

Paleontology is not, by definition, a laboratory science, and field work remains the only way to increase the fossil data, and thus to test hypotheses and refine the evolutionary models. Thom Holmes highlights some of the vibrant stories related to the art of fossil hunting, especially in the American Rockies.

Enjoy reading this volume of *The Prehistoric Earth,* and keep in mind that like mammals, concepts in paleontology are constantly evolving with new fossil discoveries and methods shedding new light on our past.

—Dr. Grégoire Métais
Muséum National d'Histoire Naturelle
UMR 5143 du CNRS
Paris, France

INTRODUCTION

The story of the evolution of the mammals, begun in the previous volume, *The Rise of Mammals,* continues in *The Age of Mammals.* Unlike the dinosaurs, whose only living relatives are birds, many of the mammal groups described in this volume are connected to living representatives across the planet today. Whereas *The Rise of the Mammals* detailed the early success and diversification of mammals following the demise of the dinosaurs, *The Age of Mammals* explores the establishment of relatively modern lines of mammals and their best-known extinct representatives.

The Rise of Mammals explained how early mammals gained a foothold on many continents during the first 10 million years of the Cenozoic Era. *The Age of Mammals* continues the story into the formative Oligocene and Miocene Epochs, a time of explosive evolutionary growth for mammals of all kinds. During this 50 million-year span, mammals not only succeeded in emerging from the shadows of the dinosaurs before them, but in becoming the most successful terrestrial vertebrates.

By the end of the age of mammals, the stage was set for the emergence of yet another species that would greatly influence the direction of life on the planet: humans. The roots of the primate family tree that spawned humans are discovered in this volume and further detailed in two other books in *The Prehistoric Earth* series, *Primates and Human Ancestors* and *Early Humans.*

OVERVIEW OF *THE AGE OF MAMMALS*

The Age of Mammals is divided into two parts covering the emergence of major evolutionary trends in mammals. Section One encompasses Extinct Marsupials, one of the two major subgroups of Theria, the group made up of mammals that give birth to live

15

young. Also known as pouched mammals, marsupials' young are born early, in a state that is little more than embryonic. The discussion of extinct marsupials is divided into two geographically based categories: the Ameridelphia (Chapter 1) of the New World (North and South America) and the Australidelphia (Chapter 2) for the Australian marsupials.

Section Two covers Extinct Eutherian Mammals. In contrast to marsupials, eutherian mammals give birth to young that have undergone an extended period of growth inside the body of the mother. Eutherians are also called "placental" mammals. The majority of modern mammals are eutherians.

The evolutionary relationships of placental mammals are sometimes murky, possibly because of the rapidity of their diversification and radiation. The discussion of eutherians is divided into several chapters covering the best-known and recognized groups and takes into account the latest work being done to understand their evolutionary relationships.

The last holdovers of the archaic eutherian mammal forms, whose lines essentially disappeared during the early part of the Cenozoic, are discussed in Chapter 3. None of these groups have any clear descendants, although convergent evolution resulted in some remarkable similarities to other mammal groups. Some of these lasted until the Pliocene Epoch, although most were extinct by the end of the Eocene. Among them were some of the most amazing browsing mammals ever seen, adorned with knobby horns and huge batteries of grinding teeth. The spectacular predator *Andrewsarchus* is also among these extinct eutherians. It was the largest known mammalian carnivore, measuring an enormous 18 feet (5.4 m) long.

The major group of living mammals and their extinct ancestors are introduced in Chapter 4 and the chapters that follow. Chapter 4 shifts to the Archonta, represented by tree shrews, flying lemurs, bats, and primates, all curiously related to one another. Within the mammal order Archonta are the primates and ancestors of humans, so it is not without special curiosity that this group is introduced.

The hoofed mammals and their extinct members are introduced in Chapter 5. One-half of all known mammalian herbivores belong to the Ungulata, or hoofed mammals. Hoofed mammals are familiar today in the forms of horses, tapirs, rhinoceroses, pigs, camels, cattle, and many other taxa. Extinct forms were equally diverse and included the largest of all known land animals, *Paraceratherium* from the Oligocene of Central Asia and Pakistan. Curiously, the whales and dolphins (order Cetacea) are also related to hoofed mammals.

The Paenungulata, consisting of the mammoths, elephants, and their relatives, is the subject of Chapter 6. Fossil remains of elephants are abundant; this is due largely to the robust nature of their bones and teeth, which are more likely than the remains of smaller animals to be preserved. The remains of mammoths that once roamed the cold northern reaches of the ice age world are sometimes found frozen with hair and organs intact. Despite the great diversity of elephants in the past, only one extant taxon remains; it includes three living species found in Africa and Asia. The Paenungulata also includes some spectacular surprises in the form of extinct marine mammals and large, horned, elephantlike browsers.

The carnivores and creodonts are explored in Chapter 7. Comprising the big cats, hyenas, dogs, bears, and their relatives, this is one of the most familiar and fascinating group of mammals. The extinct creodonts often reached spectacular proportions but were eventually supplanted by the Carnivora, whose larger brains, more adaptable dentition, and agility gave them the upper hand. The ancestors of modern carnivores date back to the Early Paleocene. These ancestors consisted of small, primitive forms that broke, very early on, into the roots of the two main groups of carnivores: the Feliformes (cats, civets, and hyenas) and the Caniformes (dogs, weasels, and bears). Among the most striking of the big cats were those with saber-tooth adaptions, a trait that is explored in detail in this chapter.

Not all eutherian mammals fit neatly into the categories discussed in the previous chapters. Chapter 8 rounds out the story of mammalian evolution by examining several remaining and equally curious groups. These include the insectivores, descendants of the earliest mammals (Insectivora); the rodents and rabbits (Glires); the pangolins (Pholidota); and the armadillos, sloths, and anteaters (Xenarthra). All of these mammal groups have living members; together, they serve as a dynamic testament to the fact that evolution can indeed favor some of the most peculiar and different kinds of organisms.

The Great Ice Age of the Pleistocene began about 2 million years ago and plunged the planet into alternating spans of icily cold and moderately warm periods. Many mammals adapted but many did not. The conclusion of *The Age of Mammals* explores the effect of the Ice Ages on mammal evolution and diversity.

The Age of Mammals builds on the same foundational principles of geology, **fossils**, and the study of life that are introduced in other volumes of *The Prehistoric Earth*. Readers who want to refresh their knowledge of certain basic terms and principles in the study of past life may wish to consult the glossary in the back of *The Age of Mammals*. Perhaps most important to keep in mind are the basic rules governing evolution: that the process of evolution is set in motion first by the traits inherited by individuals and then by the interaction of a population of a species with those traits with its habitat. Changes that enable the population to survive accumulate generation after generation, often producing and allowing species to adapt to changing conditions in the world around them. As Charles Darwin (1809–1882) explained, "The small differences distinguishing varieties of the same species steadily tend to increase, till they equal the greater differences between species of the same **genus**, or even of distinct genera." These are the rules of nature that served to stoke the engine of evolution during the Cenozoic, giving rise to forms of life whose descendants still populate Earth.

SECTION ONE:
EXTINCT MARSUPIALS

Extinct Marsupials of North and South America

Marsupials are mammals whose young are born early, in a state that is little more than embryonic. Once born, most **marsupial** offspring are suckled within the safety of a pouch. Modern examples of marsupials include kangaroos and opossums. Marsupials are one of the two major subgroups of Theria, the group made up of mammals that give birth to live young. The earliest ancestors of marsupials may have been more closely related to the egg-laying monotremes than to the extant **eutherians**, also called **placental mammals**. In addition to their reproductive traits, marsupials are distinguished from eutherians by several features in the skull and postcrania, and by having a tooth pattern that consists of three premolars and four molars. Eutherians have four or five premolars and three molars.

Living marsupials also are divided by geographic bounds; this division provides no opportunity for them to interrelate in the natural world. The two main domains of living marsupials are given the names of **Ameridelphia**, for the groups of the **New World** (North and South America), and **Australidelphia**, for the groups living of Australia.

The earliest known fossils of marsupials date from the Late Jurassic Epoch, when small, opossumlike **taxa** lived alongside dinosaurs in North America and Asia. *Alphadon* (Late Cretaceous, North America) was an omnivore capable of eating a variety of food. It is known mostly from its teeth, which resemble those of **extant** opossums. *Deltatheridium* (Late Cretaceous, Mongolia), first discovered in 1920, was for many years known only from fragments of its skull and jaw. This left its affinity with marsupials unclear. The discovery of a new set of fossil *Deltatheridium* was made in 1998. Because this set included a growth series that consisted of several excellent specimens of individuals, the discovery allowed **paleontologists** to conclude that *Deltatheridium* was indeed a marsupial. *Deltatheridium* had a short snout and an opossumlike body. The growth series in the new fossil set revealed how the animal grew and lost teeth as it matured. This knowledge enabled scientists to draw close ties to the tooth development pattern of extant marsupials.

The presence of this early marsupial in Asia during the Late Cretaceous suggests that marsupials originated in Asia before they radiated to North America and then to the Southern Hemisphere by way of South America and Australasia. All of those landmasses were still connected at the beginning of the Cenozoic Era. The story of marsupials is most remarkable in the Southern Hemisphere, where they became the dominant mammal **fauna** in some regions. In Australia, they remain the dominant fauna to this day.

Marsupials were well established by the turn of the Cenozoic Era. They were represented by no less than four families and by 19 known genera from North America alone. Most of these marsupials were small insectivores and omnivores, similar to opossums. On the threshold of the Age of Mammals, the **K-T extinction** all but wiped out the North American marsupials. This **mass extinction** left only a few remaining taxa north of the equator, but those remaining marsupials held on and persisted, living in the shadow of the eutherian mammals that took over their ecological niche.

The story was different south of the equator, where marsupials spread and thrived following the K-T extinction. They gained a foothold on several continents prior to the disappearance of the land bridges that linked them. The disappearance of the land bridges served to isolate these fauna for many millions of years. As a result of this **geographic isolation**, the marsupial faunas that arose in North America, Europe, and Asia were distinct from the faunas of South America and Australia, which proceeded along their own unique evolutionary lines. This chapter reviews the early **evolution**

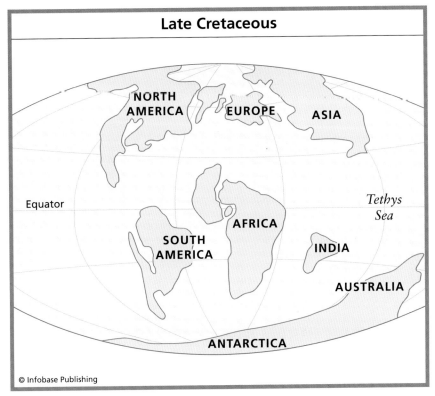

The radiation of mammals was affected by the gradually shifting configuration of the continents. Marsupials of the Southern Hemisphere became isolated either in Australia or the New World of the Americas.

of marsupials and presents the major families of extinct pouched mammals that flourished in South America. A summary of the relationships of different groups of marsupials is shown in the figure Marsupial Clades and Relationships.

The success story of marsupials was largely played out in the Southern Hemisphere. Although traces of early Cenozoic marsupials are known from north of the equator, they barely rate the attention warranted by the diversity of South American and Australian species, as evidenced by an extensive fossil record in both regions. Asian marsupials from the early Cenozoic are represented by little more than a dozen teeth found during the past 25 years. Living marsupials consist of about 265 species, two-thirds of which are

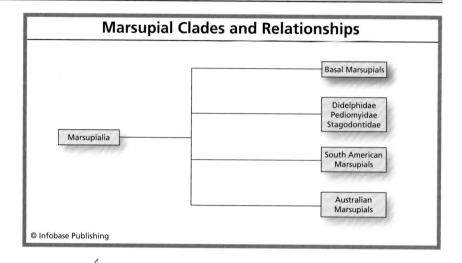

Marsupial Clades and Relationships

Marsupialia

- Basal Marsupials
- Didelphidae
  Pediomyidae
  Stagodontidae
- South American Marsupials
- Australian Marsupials

© Infobase Publishing

indigenous to Australia. Extant marsupials are classified into six groups, two from the Americas and four from Australasia.

SOUTH AMERICAN MARSUPIALS: INSECT EATERS AND PREDATORS

During the Paleocene, when the fortunes of North American marsupials were on the wane, marsupials moved to South America and experienced early success as the most prevalent mammals. The radiation of marsupials in North and South America featured a fauna that goes by the collective name Ameridelphia. Only one living member, the Virginia opossum, still lives in North America; the best-known extinct members of the group lived in South America.

Ameridelphia consists of two living and one extinct group. The Didelphimorphia, or opossums, are small to medium-sized opossums; they are the earliest known kinds of marsupials. The Paucituberculata include several families of insect-eating, **carnivorous**, and herbivorous marsupials whose origins were in South America. Today, the Paucituberculata are represented only by the shrew opossums. A third group of now-extinct marsupials was the Sparassodontia, sometimes known as the Borhyaenoidea. This group

(continues on page 28)

THINK ABOUT IT

The Migration of Early Marsupials

Marsupials became most successful in Australia, where they first appeared in the Early Eocene Epoch. Understanding the evolutionary pathway that got them there is a matter shrouded in mystery, however. The transition from the Mesozoic **Era** to the Cenozoic Era saw the last stages of the breakup of the supercontinent **Pangaea** into two land-masses, Laurasia and Gondwana. Below the equator was the landmass

(continues)

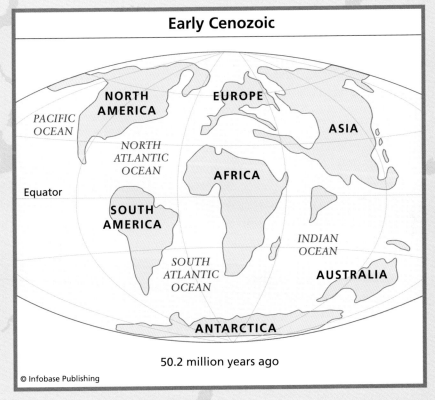

Early Cenozoic

NORTH AMERICA

EUROPE

PACIFIC OCEAN

ASIA

NORTH ATLANTIC OCEAN

AFRICA

Equator

SOUTH AMERICA

INDIAN OCEAN

SOUTH ATLANTIC OCEAN

AUSTRALIA

ANTARCTICA

50.2 million years ago

© Infobase Publishing

Map of the Early Cenozoic Era

(continued)

known as Gondwana. Gondwana eventually separated into the continents of Africa, South America, Australia, India, and Antarctica.

Africa and India were the first to make a clean break; these two landmasses then established a connection to the Northern Hemisphere through Eurasia. In the Late Cretaceous Epoch, the continents of South America, Antarctica, and Australia maintained a land bridge; but sometime between 80 million and 50 million years ago, the terrestrial link between Australia and Antarctica was lost. This isolated the fauna of Australia, which by then included ancestral marsupials.

The fossil record of marsupials is poor for the early part of the Cenozoic Era, especially in the parts of Antarctica where the presumed ancestors of Australian marsupials should be found. This gap in the fossil record has led to different theories about the origins of Australia's diverse marsupial **population**. The most likely hypothesis, supported by fossil evidence and molecular analyses, acknowledges an Asian origin of primitive marsupials during the Early Cretaceous Epoch and their subsequent geographic dispersal across the world by way of several routes, eventually leading to Australia.

Rather than migrating directly from Asia south to Australasia, it appears that marsupials spread via a more roundabout southern dispersal route. Asian marsupials first spread to Europe and North America and then from North America to South America, Antarctica, and finally Australia. In 1999, a research group led by Argentine paleontologist Francisco J. Goin identified five new **species** of primitive marsupials in middle Eocene deposits of Antarctica. This strongly suggests that the ancestors of Australian marsupials first migrated from South America to Antarctica during the early Paleocene Epoch, just after the K-T extinction.

Marsupials settled into Australia and soon diversified into six important groups. Their success in Australia was due largely to an absence of large placental mammals, especially hoofed mammals, whose role the marsupials acquired in the local ecology. Marsupials also were successful in South America, but their fortunes eventually waned in the shadow of eutherian mammals that invaded from North America. Marsupials fared much worse in North America, Europe, Asia, and Africa. Marsupials became extinct throughout most of Europe, Asia, and Africa, probably because of ecological and perhaps climatic reasons, but an exception is found in North America.

The only marsupial found in North America today is the Virginia opossum. This primitive descendant of early marsupials did not originate above the equator, however. The first line of opossumlike marsupials that arose in North America in the early Cenozoic became extinct by the Miocene Epoch. The line was reintroduced from South America later, about 3.5 million years ago, when a land bridge—the Great American Interchange—formed temporarily between South America and North America.

The Virginia opossum is the only still-living North American marsupial.

(continued from page 24)

consisted of two subgroups of large carnivorous mammals. Fossil marsupials are found in only a few select localities in South America. These include areas in Bolivia, Peru, Brazil, and the Patagonian badlands of Argentina.

Remains of extinct South American marsupials reach back to the Paleocene, but there is little certainty about exactly how far back the line goes. The earliest known marsupial is from China, the exquisitely preserved *Sinodelphys* (Early Cretaceous, China). *Sinodelphys* is known from a nearly complete skeleton that shows evidence of fur tufts. This rodentlike marsupial measured only about 6 inches (15 cm) long, and it probably was tree living. The *Sinodelphys* body plan and its lifestyle of scurrying across trees and bushes in search of small insects and worms probably were echoed in the first marsupials to arise in South America.

Didelphimorphia: The Opossums

The Didelphimorphia are small to medium-sized opossums characterized by a classic, though primitive, dental formula. Didelphimorphs have small incisors and large canines and a molar formula that consists of three premolars and four molars with three cusps. The skull typically has a long snout, and the tail is prehensile: It is adapted for grasping. Active mostly at night, didelphimorphs, including extinct species, probably are **omnivorous** or opportunistic feeders, choosing insects, plants, or possibly carrion as food sources. Didelphimorphs first arose in Asia. They migrated to North America and then to South America and Antarctica. In the north, a few didelphimorphs are known from Europe and also from northern Africa. They were the only form of marsupial to make an appearance in northern Africa.

Szalinia (Paleocene, Bolivia). This small opossum was found in the earliest mammal fossil beds of South America. It shared its habitat with early placental mammals. Eleven taxa of marsupials are known from this locality, including *Pucadelphys*, the best representative of the group and known by several exquisitely preserved and complete skeletons. The position of *Szalinia* in the evolution of the marsupials is intriguing. *Szalinia* has a jaw design that appears to fit in between the jaw designs of early North American didelphimorphs, such as *Kokopellia*, and the jaw designs of more typical opossumlike creatures found at this Bolivian site. *Szalinia* therefore represents an intermediate stage of evolution between the early marsupials of North America and South America and so provides support for the theory that the southern radiation of marsupials originated above the equator. *Szalinia* was small, with an upper jaw that measured only about 2 inches (5 cm) long.

Pucadelphys (Paleocene, Bolivia). One of the best-known didelphimorphs of South America is *Pucadelphys*; evidence for this animal includes partial and complete skeletons. The upper jaw of *Pucadelphys*, including the long canine teeth typical of opossums, was only about 3 inches (7.5 cm) long. This attests to the tiny size of the early marsupials. Analysis of the **hind limbs** of *Pucadelphys* suggests that it was more agile than modern opossums and probably more sure-footed while climbing and walking on uneven surfaces. *Pucadelphys* was not as well adapted for climbing as is the Virginia opossum. Some specimens of *Pucadelphys* have been found in pairs, apparently having perished together in a nest, perhaps buried in a burrow by a deluge of mud.

Sparassocynus (Miocene to Pleistocene, Bolivia and Argentina). Another curious didelphimorph from South America was *Sparassocynus*. It is known from an excellent skull that shows a somewhat shorter snout than is typical of opossums. The skull is bulbous behind the eyes, particularly in the area of the ear; the purpose of such specialization is unknown. The teeth of *Sparassocynus* provide a further mystery, with molars that have been modified for more efficient slicing, possibly for a diet that leaned more toward meat than plants.

Paucituberculata: Insect and Plant Eaters

This group of marsupials from South America includes the living shrew opossums. The extinct members of this family form a diverse group that includes 12 families that were so different from one another that the key traits shared by all were their characteristically broad molar teeth and the development of forward-facing lower incisor and canine teeth. Early members of the group date from the Paleocene and include the small, insect-eating *Roberthoffestetteria* (Paleocene, Bolivia). Some of the better-known paucituberculates lived during the Oligocene, Miocene, and Pliocene Epochs.

Epidolops (Late Paleocene, Brazil). One of the earliest known members of the paucituberculates was *Epidolops*, known from nearly complete but crushed skull and jaw elements. With a skull that was only about 3.5 inches (9 cm) long, the dentition of this insect eater included elongated and forward-facing lower incisors that could have been used to scoop insects and small invertebrates such as worms from the soil. Most curious were the lower premolars of *Epidolops*, which had a tall cusp and a bladelike edge.

Groeberia (Late Eocene to Early Oligocene, Argentina). This little marsupial from Argentina had a skull like that of no other mammal. It had a short, flattened snout with an almost rabbitlike appearance. Its teeth were uniquely suited for crushing nuts and other hard food. At the anterior joint, where the two halves of the lower jaw met, *Groeberia* had a flat, bony surface that extended back into the floor of the mouth; this presumably was a surface for crushing hard food. *Groeberia* had enormous, rodentlike incisors on the upper jaws and a broad, single incisor on the lower jaw. The incisors were self-sharpening as the animal gnawed. Immediately behind the incisors, near the front of the mouth, were premolars. *Groeberia* evidently had a bit of an overbite, and the upper set of premolars was positioned so that they could grind food against the upper surface of the single, broad lower incisor. Nothing else of the skeleton has been found to date, making the head of *Groeberia* the only part that is understood. The dentition, strange as it might be, contains a dental formula for premolars and molars that clearly associates this unusual mammal with the marsupials.

Argyrolagus (Pliocene, Argentina). This small marsupial was first known from a partial skull that led paleontologists to conclude that its buck teeth belonged to an ancient rodent. Later specimens drew a different picture as the particulars of the jaws and skull of *Argyrolagus* became clear. Although unrelated to rodents, *Argyrolagus* nonetheless had the appearance of a kangaroo rat, a case of **convergent evolution** among early mammals. Measuring about 16 inches (40 cm) long including its lengthy tail, *Argyrolagus* had short legs and long, two-toed feet that allowed it to hop about. It was a quick-moving insect eater with a long-snouted head and an overbite containing the protruding incisors characteristic of this early family of marsupials.

Sparassodontia: Large Carnivorous Marsupials

In contrast to other South American marsupials, the Sparassondonta were larger, carnivorous creatures that resembled bears, dogs, and large cats more than typical marsupials. This entirely extinct group filled a predatory niche occupied by placental mammals in the Northern Hemisphere and Africa. Two families of sparassondonts thrived in South America from the Paleocene to the early Pliocene, where they eventually were displaced by an invasion of placental mammals from the north.

One family of sparassondonts was the borhyaenids, short-limbed and stout-bodied **predators** with doglike skulls and teeth. The second family of sparassondonts was the thylacosmilids. These were carnivorous hunters whose skulls are very catlike and resemble the skulls of saber-toothed cats, with extremely long upper canine teeth. The molars of both of these families were modified for shearing meat. Neither of these groups of sparassodonts was related to placental mammals found on other continents, such as bears, cats, and dogs; their similarities are attributable purely to convergent evolution.

Sparassodonts reached their peak of diversity during the Miocene, from which more than two dozen taxa are known. Although the extensive fossil record of sparassodonts suggests that they were successful predators, they were by no means the top or largest predators of the day. That distinction was held by large, flightless, predatory birds such as *Phorusrhacos* (Early to Middle Miocene, Argentina). These birds towered even over the sparasodonts and possibly competed with them for food.

Prothylacinus (Paleocene, Argentina). This small sparassondont predator had a body that measured about 31 inches (80 cm) long. The animal had a flat, low-to-the-ground posture somewhat like that of a fox and a head that resembled that of a long-snouted cat. *Prothylacinus* was flat-footed, or **plantigrade**—a trait of more primitive marsupials that probably limited its quickness and maneuverability on uneven surfaces.

Borhyaena (Late Oligocene to Early Miocene, Argentina). *Borhyaena* had a body length of about 5 feet (1.5 m), making it similar to a puma or jaguar in size. It had a boxy, bearlike skull with long canine teeth for killing prey. This large animal with short legs was probably not a fast runner. It perhaps relied on ambushing its prey, cutting out weaker members of the local hoofed mammal groups abundant in its environment, or scavenging dead animals.

Thylacosmilus (Late Miocene to Early Pliocene, Argentina). *Thylacosmilus* was the longest-surviving member of the sparassondonts and probably competed with placental mammals that were invading from the north by the time of the Pliocene Epoch. In many respects, *Thylacosmilus* is best described as resembling the better-known saber-toothed cats of North America, although it was totally unrelated to placental mammals. This fairly large animal had a body that measured about 4 feet (1.2 m) long. Its most remarkable feature was a pair of extremely long upper canine teeth that it used to kill its prey. The jaw joint was modified so that it could open at nearly a 90-degree angle, to allow *Thylacosmilus* to open its mouth wide. The anterior portion of the lower jaw was itself long and protruded downward; it provided open grooves on either side in which the canines of *Thylacosmilus* could rest when the mouth was closed. Unlike the teeth of the saber-toothed cats, the canines of *Thylacosmilus* grew continuously throughout the animal's life. *Thylacosmilus* had no incisors.

Theories about how *Thylacosmilus* and other "saber-toothed" predators used their enormous canines have been a matter of speculation for many years. The prevailing idea was expressed by American paleontologist William Berryman Scott (1858–1947) when, in 1913, he first suggested that "the only way in which the sabers could have been effectively used was by striking a downward, stabbing blow with the whole head." Recent refinements of this idea have suggested that the teeth could have been used to puncture, hold, and drag down running prey; to strike at a prey animal's softer underbelly; or perhaps to stab and grab a prey animal's neck until it suffocated from having its esophagus crushed.

THE RISE AND FALL OF SOUTH AMERICAN MARSUPIALS

Following the K-T extinction, marsupials from the Northern Hemisphere migrated to South America, where they radiated quickly and with great diversity during the early part of the Cenozoic Era. Except for traces of ancestral taxa above the equator, the marsupials of North America, Europe, and Asia appear to have dwindled early due in part to competition from the eutherian mammals that rapidly dominated these habitats.

In South America, the marsupial story took a different direction. Arriving before the widespread radiation of eutherian mammals, marsupials quickly dominated the ecological niches for mammalian fauna of South America. There they remained, relatively undisturbed and unchanged, as South America became geographically isolated from North America during most of the Cenozoic. During the Pliocene Epoch, however, a land bridge was reestablished between the Americas. This allowed placental mammals to migrate south. This migration was the undoing of South American marsupials, whose less advanced taxa could not compete effectively with the stronger, quicker, and more varied mammals from the North. Most South American marsupials are now extinct, as are marsupials in most of the northern continents.

SUMMARY

This chapter reviewed the early evolution of marsupials and presented the major families of extinct pouched mammals that flourished in South America.

1. All marsupials in the Americas comprise a fauna that goes by the collective name Ameridelphia.
2. The earliest fossil record of marsupials is from the Early Cretaceous of China, and by the end of the Mesozoic marsupials had migrated to North America and then to South America.
3. Two living groups within the Ameridelphia include the Didelphimorphia, or opossums, and the Paucituberculata, a group that consists of several families of insect-eating, carnivorous, and herbivorous marsupials.
4. The Sparassodontia, sometimes known as the Borhyaenoidea, is an extinct group within Ameridelphia that included two groups of large, carnivorous marsupials.
5. Fossil marsupials are found in only a few select localities in South America, including Bolivia, Peru, Brazil, and the Patagonian badlands of Argentina.

EXTINCT MARSUPIALS OF AUSTRALIA

Early marsupials had no greater success than in Australia. Arriving somewhat later, and linked to the first marsupials of North America and South America, Australian marsupials were geologically isolated from the rest of the world during most of their reign. This enabled them to dominate the local mammalian fauna in a way unlike marsupials anywhere else on the globe. As a testament to the success of the marsupials of Australia, about 200 of the nearly 265 living species of extant marsupials worldwide live exclusively in Australia today, where they continue to dominate the wild fauna. This chapter traces the roots of the Australian marsupials and explores many extraordinary examples of extinct taxa that range from shrewlike omnivores to lion-sized predators.

AUSTRALIAN MARSUPIALS: CONQUEST OF THE POUCHED MAMMALS

Australia was geographically isolated from other continents during most of the Age of Mammals. The seeds of Australian mammalian evolution arrived on the island continent early in the Cenozoic, when Australia was still connected to Antarctica and Antarctica was linked to South America. That link vanished early in the Age of Mammals, however. The severing of the link left the mammals of Australia to evolve their own peculiar traits and led to their great success in most ecological niches on the continent.

The early marsupials of Australia apparently did not face competition from eutherian mammals as did marsupials on other

continents. Instead, the marsupials of Australia became the dominant clan of mammals. The variety of Australian pouched mammals was greater than on any other continent. The animals ranged
widely in size, in body plan, and in lifestyle. So successful were
the marsupials in Australia that they comprised nearly every kind
of mammal that lived on the continent until the latter half of the
Cenozoic Era.

Because the fossil record of early Cenozoic Australian mammals is poor, few parallels can be made between the early radiation
of mammals in North America, Europe, Asia, and South America
and the Paleocene fauna of Australia. The fossil record of Australian marsupials begins around the early Eocene but continues to be
spotty until the late Oligocene and Miocene, when an abundance of
evidence first appears.

The term Australidelphia is given to the clade comprising all
Australian marsupials, but this group is not restricted geographically to Australia. These animals are considered to be a related
group that is descended from a common ancestor. The marsupials
of Australia are made up of six groups, all but one of which still has
living descendants. These groups include the extinct Yalkaparidontia (small eaters of worms and insects); Microbiotheria (the only
known Australian group that is directly related to an extinct South
American **taxon**); Dasyuromorphia (carnivorous marsupials); Notoryctemorphia (marsupial moles); Peramelemorphia (bandicoots and
bilbies); and Diprotodontia (kangaroos, wallabies, and wombats).
Extinct members of these groups are introduced below.

Yalkaparidontia

This extinct group of Australian marsupials is known only from
a single taxon: *Yalkaparidon* (Early Miocene, Australia), or "boomerang tooth." The boomerang shape of its molars, formed by
prominent cusps, is the inspiration for the animal's name, which
combines the aboriginal word for boomerang and the Greek word
for tooth. First described in 1988 by a paleontological team led by
Michael Archer of the University of New South Wales, *Yalkaparidon*

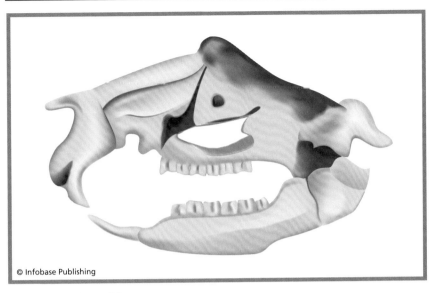

© Infobase Publishing

Skull of a *Yalkaparidon*

had a skull length of only about 2 inches (5 cm). It also had a reduced dental formula for a marsupial that included large upper and lower incisors and the unusual shape of the molars mentioned above.

Yalkaparidon's incisors grew continuously, and the animal had an unusual overbite. This has led to some speculation about the diet of this little pouched mammal. The prevailing theory is that its large incisors were used to puncture or gnaw at small invertebrates such as shelled insects or worms. Its molars, with their severe, V-shaped crest, would not have been suited for the grinding of hard food. This suggests that the diet of *Yalkaparidon* consisted mainly of soft tissue, perhaps extracted from an invertebrate exoskeleton. *Yalkaparidon* lived in lowland rainforest areas of northern Australia until that habitat disappeared in the latter part of the Cenozoic Era.

Microbiotheria

The Australidelphia form a related clade of exclusively Australian marsupials with the exception of one outlying group, the microbiotheres. This group has one living species, *Dromiciops*, that is found in beech and bamboo forests of South America. Also known by the name *monito del monte* ("little mountain monkey"), *Dromiciops* and its extinct South American ancestors from Bolivia, Argentina, and Antarctica appear to be more closely related to Australian marsupials than to the marsupials of South America. This connection probably was made through a migration path that led from Australasia to Antarctica and that was still intact during the Early Paleocene Epoch. Remains of possible extinct microbiotheres of Australia have been reported but not yet formally described by paleontologists. *Dromiciops* is a mouse-sized tree climber with large eyes; a coat of dense, silky fur; and a prehensile tail. The animal feeds on insects and other small invertebrates.

Dasyuromorphia: Predators with Pouches

The dasyuromorphs include three groups of carnivorous marsupials. The living Dasyuridae comprise animals that range in size from that of a mole to that of a large cat. All living Dasyuridae have a similar body plan, however, with a long snout, sharp canine teeth, a plantigrade posture, and a furry tail that is not prehensile. Tasmanian devils and quolls are two examples of populous living dasyurids. A few fossil representatives of this group are known, including *Barinya* (Late Oligocene to Early Miocene, Australia).

A second living group of dasyurids is the Myrmecobiidae, a group known today from one taxon, the living numbat (or banded anteater). This is a small, bushy-tailed ground dweller that specializes in eating termites with its long snout. To date, no extinct fossil members of this group are known.

The third group of dasyurids is the Thylacinidae, a recently extinct group comprising the largest Australian carnivorous marsupials. The fossil record of extinct thylacinids represents a somewhat diverse group of predators that lived from the Late Oligocene onward. A spurt of discoveries during the past 15 years has brought the number of known thylacinid to six genera and eight species. This has added much to the understanding of this group.

Badjcinus (Early Oligocene, Australia) was a cat-size thylacinid and one of the earliest known members of the group. *Badjcinus* is

Thylacinus was closely related to *Badjcinus*.

the most primitive, least **derived** member of the thylacinids and is known primarily from partial jaw and skull fossils. It has been likened to the living tiger quoll, a cat-sized, arboreal (tree-dwelling), insect-eating marsupial still found in Australia.

In the study of mammals, it sometimes is possible for paleontologists to learn about fossil animals by studying closely related living species. Such is the case with the taxon *Thylacinus* (Early Miocene to present), the Tasmanian tiger. This animal was known until the twentieth century; the last known member of the group died in captivity in 1936, at the Hobart Zoo in Tasmania, Australia. Earlier members of this recently extinct taxon were much like the specimens that lived until the 1930s, but with some notable differences. Miocene members of the genus were stockier and had a shorter snout and broader skull than modern species. The teeth of the Miocene *Thylacinus* were not as highly specialized for shearing meat as were the teeth of the modern species, but both animals shared the same dental formula.

Notoryctemorphia: Marsupial Moles

The small, burrowing mammals known as marsupial moles live today in the deserts of Western Australia. Although the body plan of the marsupial mole is strikingly similar to that of eutherian moles, and to that of the African golden mole in particular, these similarities are the consequence of convergent evolution rather than of any close evolutionary ties with placental mammals. Living marsupial moles are blind, have burrowing paws, lack external ear appendages, and have a sausagelike body covered with fine hair. The largest they get is about 6.25 inches (16 cm) long. Their pouch faces backward; this ensures that the pouch doesn't collect sand when the animal burrows. *Notoryctes* is the only known genus of living marsupial moles.

Fossil traces of marsupial moles are rare; they consist only of isolated teeth and skeletal fragments from Oligocene and Miocene fossil deposits of northwestern Australia. One thing appears certain, however: The marsupial moles have an ancient history that seems to parallel that of the most ancient Australian mammal fauna.

Peramelemorphia: Bandicoots and Bilbies

The peramelemorphs include about 20 living species of small mouse- and rat-sized omnivores, commonly called bandicoots and bilbies. They have long snouts, arching backs, long tails, and long hind limbs with two fused toes that are somewhat like those of kangaroos, though the bandicoots and bilbies are not directly related to kangaroos. The presence in the peramelemorphs' lower front jaw of several pairs of teeth is reminiscent of the dasyuromorph carnivorous marsupials, while the limbs and feet of the peramelemorphs share features with the diprotodont kangaroos and wallabies. Whatever the roots of the peramelemorph family, the earliest extinct members of the group appeared in the Late Oligocene and Miocene and were quite populous during those times.

Yarala (Late Oligocene to Early Miocene, Australia) was first described in 1995 based on a skull fossil from northwestern Australia. It most resembles the modern bandicoot. It is sometimes described as a "tube-nosed" bandicoot because of its long, narrow

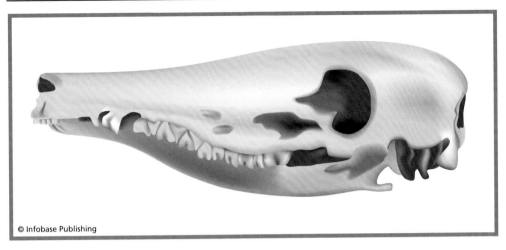

© Infobase Publishing

A *Peramelemorph* skull

skull. Measuring about 18 inches (45 cm) from head to tail, the taxon is known from an excellently preserved skull and numerous other skeletal fragments.

Diprotodontia: Giant Kangaroos, Wallabies, and Wombats

The largest group of Australian marsupials was the diprotodonts. This varied clade includes three living groups: the Vombatiformes (koalas and wombats); the Phalageriformes (Australian opossums); and the Macropodiformes (kangaroos and wallabies). The group also included several other groups of extinct herbivorous marsupials. The evolutionary history of the diprotodonts extends back to their first appearance during the Late Oligocene; several modern groups did not appear until as recently as the Holocene, some 10,000 years ago. As many as 16 different groups of diprotodonts have been recognized, many of which were extinct by the post-Miocene span of the Cenozoic Era. Living diprotodonts include about 120 species of kangaroos, opossums, wallabies, koalas, and wombats.

The name diprotodonts refers to one of the traits shared by all members of the clade: a pair of large, forward-pointing incisors on the lower jaw. In addition, the second and third digits of the hind feet

Koalas are a living species of diprotodonts.

of diprotodonts are fused except for the claws, which remain separate at the tip of the joined toes. Other modifications of the feet include a greatly enlarged fourth digit and a small or nearly absent fifth digit.

The fossil record for prehistoric diprotodonts is spotty, with some families known only from teeth and other disassociated fragments that hint at their marsupial affinities. Extinct members of some of the key orders of diprotodonts are described below.

Wynyardiidae

Fossils of this extinct group of diprotodonts have been found in deposits that date from the Late Oligocene and Early Miocene. These dog-sized marsupial specimens represent some of the most primitive of the wynyardiids—they had simple, unspecialized feet; short legs; and robust molars operated by relatively simple jaw mechanics. This possibly indicates a reduction in biting strength when compared with some other, more specialized **herbivores**.

Muramura (Late Oligocene to Early Miocene, Australia). *Muramura* is well known from at least two complete specimens and many jaw and skull elements. Its large cheek premolars and molars were sharply cusped and relatively similar in shape, thus providing a generalized dental battery for handling a variety of vegetation. The anterior tip of the jaws converged to a point and was capped by two long, forwardly directed upper and lower incisors.

Diprotodontidae

This group of mostly cow-sized Australian marsupials lived from the Late Oligocene to recent times in the Late Pleistocene. The animals were large and bulky and possessed plantigrade feet and a lower leg bone that was shorter than the upper leg bone. These are indications that these animals were ponderously slow movers; they probably were grazing animals and browsers that dug up roots and other vegetation from fields and forest floors. Some had high nasal openings, suggesting a large bump on the top of the snout. In evolutionary terms, the diprotodonts were oversized ancestors of wombats and were the largest marsupials ever to exist. Whereas

A *Diprotodon* skull

extant wombats grow to about the size of a beaver, some extinct diprotodonts were as large as a hippopotamus and weighed nearly 3 tons (2.7 metric tons).

Diprotodon (Late Pleistocene, Australia). *Diprotodon* was a giant even among diprotodonts. It measured up to 10 feet (3 m) long and stood more than 8 feet (2.6 m) tall at the hump of the back. Its molars were large and well adapted for eating soft vegetation and possibly water plants. The *Diprotodon* skull was massive, and its upper jaw contained forward-pointing incisors that were probably hidden by a fleshy snout. *Diprotodon*'s front feet were well adapted for digging up plants. The animal probably rooted up plants with its claws and its tusklike incisors and then ground the plant matter to a pulp with its massive cheek molars.

Neohelos (Late Oligocene to Early Miocene, Australia). Known from an abundance of jaws, skulls, and informative **postcranial** skeletons, this herbivore was most abundant during the Early Miocene and probably lived in herds like cattle. *Neohelos* is similar to members of the group known as the Diprotodontidae, but

Diprotodon (Late Pleistocene, Australia) probably rooted up plants with its claws and its tusklike incisors and then ground the plant matter to a pulp with its massive cheek molars.

Neohelos is distinguished by a particular derived cusp shape found on its teeth alone.

Macropodidae

This subgroup of the diprotodonts includes the living kangaroos, whose evolutionary roots reach back to several taxa of extinct ancestors.

Procoptodon (Pleistocene, Australia). This was the largest kangaroo that ever lived. It measured about 10 feet (3 m) long and stood about 6.5 feet (2 m) tall. Of its four hind toes, only the enlarged, fourth toe was functionally weight bearing, and all the toes were fused together by tissue. Such fused toes are still seen in modern kangaroos, although toes two and three of modern taxa are longer than the same toes in extinct ancestors. *Procoptodon* undoubtedly was a good hopper like the modern kangaroo. Its skull had a shorter snout than that seen in modern kangaroos. *Procoptodon* had powerful jaws and grinding molars to chew tough grasses and other vegetation in its plains environment. Its large size, powerful limbs, and speed probably enabled it to defend itself vigorously against predators, all of which were smaller.

Palorchestidae

This group consists of large, herbivorous quadrupeds with an appearance most like that of living tapirs. Tapirs are unrelated to palorchestids, however. At one time, palorchestids were considered to be diprotodonts, but the palorchestids differ in several features of the skull and dentition. These differences make the palorchestids more closely related to living wombats.

Palorchestes (Late Pleistocene, Australia). This animal was the size of a small horse. It had burly **forelimbs** and had long, bearlike claws on its feet. The front claws were particularly long. These claws presumably were used to dig up roots and tubers and perhaps to pull down branches from trees. The nostril region of the skull indicates that *Palorchestes*, whose name means "marsupial tapir," may have had a short trunk similar to that of living tapirs. *Palorchestes* measured about 8 feet (2.5 m) long.

Thylacoleonidae

In addition to the many varieties of browsing, plant-eating marsupials of Australia's past, there existed another group of related predators that reigned over the Australian grasslands from the Late Oligocene to the Pleistocene Epoch. Known as the "marsupial lions," these intriguing offshoots of Australian mammals were descendants of herbivorous forebears. Extinct thylacoleonids are most closely related to wombats and koalas. Thylacoleonids ranged in size from that of a cat to that of a moderately large lion. The predatory specialization of their teeth took the form of forward-pointing, pointed incisors that the animals used somewhat in the manner of the daggerlike canines found in true cats.

Priscileo (Late Oligocene to Middle Miocene, Australia). *Priscileo* was a small thylacoleonid about the size of a large cat. Its jaws

In this illustration, the two large, bearlike mammals are *Diprotodon*; the mammals with tapirlike trunks at center are *Palorchestes*; and the mammals in the foreground are *Zygomaturus*.

contained a combination of sharp-edged molars for slicing flesh and blunt molars for crushing or chewing. This suggests that this most primitive of thylacoleonids may have been omnivorous and opportunistic in its diet preferences. *Priscileo* may have preferred to scavenge dead animals rather than to pursue live prey. Its **anatomy** also suggests that it may have lived much of the time in trees. Nearly complete skulls have been discovered for *Priscileo.*

Wakaleo (Middle to Late Miocene, Australia). This thylacoleonid was about as big as a medium-sized dog. Its teeth were specialized for stabbing and cutting. *Wakaleo* stalked its prey both on the ground and in the trees of the Miocene forests of Australia. The animal is well known from numerous fossils specimens, including partial skulls. *Wakaleo* measured about 2.5 feet (0.75 m) long.

Thylacoleo (Pliocene to Pleistocene, Australia). This was by far the largest of the marsupial lions; it measured about 6.5 feet (2 m) long. Its tall skull, pointed incisors, and flesh-shearing cheek teeth combined with powerful jaw muscles to make *Thylacoleo* a fierce predator. Recent studies of the bite force of *Thylacoleo* indicate that it fed on large prey such as the bulky diprotodonts that shared its grassy plains. Its biting strategy was much like that of today's large cats: It used its pointed front teeth (canines, in actual cats) and long-edged premolars to bite and then shear away flesh. *Thylacoleo* also had a pair of thumblike claws that it possibly used to grasp and disembowel its prey. This leopard-sized animal probably weighed about 285 pounds (130 kg) but had a bite force equal to that of the living African lion, an animal that can weigh 550 pounds (250 kg). *Thylacoleo* had a stronger bite than any other known mammal, living or extinct.

SUCCESS AND DIVERSITY OF AUSTRALIAN MARSUPIALS

The continued success of Australian marsupials is due in large part to the isolation of the land down under and its associated neighbors, New Zealand and New Guinea. Despite the eventual introduction of placental mammals into Australia, the evolutionary roots and diversity of Australian marsupials were great enough to withstand competition from eutherians—a success story quite different from the fate of marsupials on other continents.

Australian marsupials of the Middle Cenozoic Era faced rapid changes in climate that required them to adapt more quickly than their South American cousins. As Australia separated from Antartica and moved northward, its climate changed from that of a temperate zone to that of a tropical zone. This affected the lifestyles and adaptations of its native marsupials. The stresses and successes of such rapid diversification were contributing factors to the continued success of Australian marsupials. When eutherian mammals finally showed up in force in Australia, the native marsupials were more than up to the task of holding their own.

SUMMARY

This chapter traced the roots of the Australian marsupials and explored many extraordinary examples of extinct taxa.

1. The term Australidelphia is given to the clade that comprises all Australian marsupials.
2. Australian marsupials are considered to be a related group that is descended from a common ancestor.
3. The marsupials of Australia are made up of six groups, all but one of which still has living descendants.
4. These groups include the extinct Yalkaparidontia (small eaters of worms and insects); Microbiotheria (the only known Australian group that is directly related to an extinct South American taxon); Dasyuromorphia (carnivorous marsupials); Notoryctemorphia (marsupial moles); Peramelemorphia (bandicoots and bilbies); and Diprotodontia (kangaroos, wallabies, and wombats).
5. Australian marsupials owe some of their evolutionary success to the need to adapt quickly to widespread changes to the Australian climate. This ability to adapt to change made them heartier and less prone to competition from invading placental mammals.

SECTION TWO:
EXTINCT EUTHERIAN MAMMALS

LAST OF THE ARCHAIC EUTHERIANS

In contrast to marsupials, eutherian mammals give birth to young that have undergone an extended period of growth inside the body of the mother. Eutherians are also called "placental" mammals, after the placenta, a temporary organ found in females during the gestation of an embryo. The majority of modern mammals are eutherians, but the interrelationships remain poorly understood. This suggests that the diversification of these groups from an ancestral stock occurred very rapidly, probably right after the events of the transition marked by the K-T extinction. Despite the many diverse kinds of eutherians, all members of the group are diagnosed by a series of morphological features, including a tooth pattern that comprises only three molars and a distinctive cusp pattern.

Early eutherians were well established in North America, Central Asia, and Asia during the latter part of the Mesozoic Era, when the first placental mammals coexisted with the dinosaurs. The oldest known eutherian mammal is *Eomaia* (Early Cretaceous, China), the "dawn mother." Small enough to fit in the palm of one's hand, *Eomaia* was discovered in the same famous fossil lake beds of China that are known for many remains of small, feathered dinosaurs; birds; plants; and the largest known archaic Mesozoic mammal, the dinosaur-eating *Repenomamus*.

Eomaia was found on a rock slab that also preserved the outline of its thick furry coat. It was only mouse sized: about 6 inches (16 cm) long including its tail. It had long fingers and claws that could wrap around the branches that it climbed; these adaptations

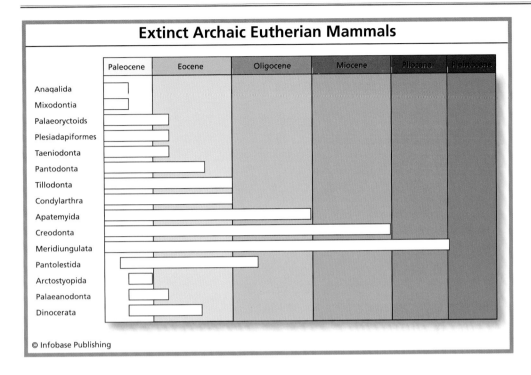

Extinct Archaic Eutherian Mammals

© Infobase Publishing

made it highly specialized for this task. Although the teeth and limbs of *Eomaia* strongly resemble those of later eutherians, the narrow pelvis of this mammal suggests that young were born quite small and perhaps not entirely as well developed as those of later placentals. Another primitive eutherian was *Zalambdalestes* (Late Cretaceous, Mongolia), a small, insect-eating quadruped with an upturned snout that resembled that of a shrew.

The foundation of modern mammal groups was well established by the end of the Mesozoic. Several groups of early eutherians survived the K-T transition but became extinct in the early part of the Cenozoic. None of these groups has any clear descendants, although convergent evolution resulted in some remarkable similarities to other mammal groups. These archaic eutherians were remarkable in their variety of sizes, appearances, and lifestyles. They provide an early glimpse at the potential success of eutherian mammals that continues to this day.

This chapter reviews several key groups of extinct eutherian mammals that dominated life on land during the first part of the Cenozoic Era. The span during which they evolved is illustrated in the diagram Extinct Archaic Eutherian Mammals.

TAENIODONTS: TREE-CLIMBERS AND DIGGERS

The Taeniodonta included omnivorous tree climbers and diggers that lived in North America from the Early Paleocene to the Early Eocene. The taeniodont body was stout, with short limbs and a muscular skull. The earliest members of this group were more opossumlike, with large upper and lower canines and cheek molars for shearing and grinding food. The dentition of taeniodonts evolved rapidly during the short span of their reign. Some later taxa were boar-sized, with tall, blunt skulls and powerful jaws fronted by enlarged incisors and canines.

Onychodectes (Early Paleocene, North America). This tree climber was the size of a large cat and was one of the earliest taeniodonts. Its long, low skull had jaws equipped with somewhat long upper and lower canines. Its leaf-shaped premolars and short, blunt molars were widely spaced. The limbs of *Onychodectes* were stout and muscular, particularly the forelimbs. The forelimbs also were equipped with robust claws and flexible wrist joints, both of which enabled this mammal to dig and climb with equal proficiency.

Stylinodon (Early Eocene, North America). *Stylinodon* differed in many respects from the earlier taeniodont *Onychodectes*, even though *Stylinodon* lived not too long afterward. This is an example of the rapid evolution and radiation of this mammal clan. *Stylinodon* was the largest of this early mammal group; it reached about 4.5 feet (1.4 m) in length and had a stout, piglike body. Its heavy skull had a broad snout and highly specialized dentition. Whereas *Onychodectes* had relatively slender canines and unremarkable incisors, *Stylinodon* had developed greatly enlarged and widened canines and incisors positioned in the front of its jaw to form a massive gnawing mechanism. The incisors and canines of *Stylinodon* were rootless, and they grew continuously. This suggests that they were used to chisel or gnaw tough vegetation, much like the teeth of rodents and rabbits. The molars, too, were significantly larger than in earlier taeniodonts and were topped with high crowns to improve their abrasive characteristics. *Stylinodon*'s legs were short, and its feet were equipped with long claws for uprooting tubers and other vegetation.

PANTODONTA: EARLY LARGE BROWSERS

Pantodonta were some of the first large eutherian mammals to appear in the Cenozoic. Early forms lived in China during the Early Paleocene, and their first occurrence in North America appears to have been in the Middle to Late Paleocene. Most pantodonts ranged in size from that of a rat to that of a dog, but the group also represented the first large browsing mammals in the form of *Coryphodon* (Middle Eocene, North America), an animal that was about 7.5 feet (2.25 m) long—the size of a large bear. The smallest pantodonts, such as *Achaeolambda*, possibly were arboreal, while some of the bulkier taxa, such as the slothlike *Barylambda*, may have been more hippopotamuslike and semiaquatic. Among the earliest pantodonts is *Alcidedorbignya* (Early Paleocene, Bolivia), an animal that provides an early link between eutherian mammals of North America and those of South America.

Bemalambda (Early Paleocene, China). *Bemalambda* is one of the earliest known pantodonts; it is understood from several fossil skulls and partial skeletons. As a suggestion of things to come for pantodonts, even this early member of the group was moderately large, about the size of a big dog, with a skull that measured about 8 inches (21 cm) long. The teeth of *Bemalambda* were typical of pantodonts, with small canines and a set of closely spaced premolars and molars. The molars of *Bemalambda* had V-shaped cross ridges, or lophs—a distinguishing feature that separates the most primitive pantodonts from later taxa, the molars of which had W-shaped lophs. The skeleton of this early browsing animal was more lightly built than that of the taeniodonts, with longer legs.

Titanoides (Late Paleocene, North America). The bearlike *Titanoides* was about 5 feet (1.5 m) long, with a large, muscular head and a short torso. Its front legs and feet were adapted for digging, and its broad back had a slight ridge down the center. Its dental battery included two large upper canines that overlapped the lower jaw when the mouth was closed, like small tusks. Despite its ferocious appearance, *Titanoides*, like other pantodonts, was a browsing plant eater.

Coryphodon (Middle Eocene, North America). *Coryphodon* represented yet another variation on the pantodont body plan. Measuring about 7.5 feet (2.25 m) long, *Coryphodon* had a stocky build like a tapir or hippopotamus. Its feet were hoofed rather than clawed—a convergent adaptation outside of the family line normally associated with true hoofed mammals. Canine tusks dropped from the sides of *Coryphodon*'s upper jaw and may have been used to grasp and uproot plants. The robust molars of *Coryphodon* were equipped with W-shaped lophs and were well suited for eating soft tropical plants. It is thought that this animal may have led a partly aquatic lifestyle.

CONDYLARTHRA: EARLY HOOFED MAMMALS

The Condylarthra were a group of **basal** hoofed mammals, or **ungulates**, from the early Cenozoic; they represent the early radiation of ungulates. The condylarths included some of the most common mammals from the Early Paleocene to Late Eocene of North America, Europe, and Asia. It is unlikely that the condylarths as a whole were descended from a common ancestor. This group included small and mostly primitive herbivores as well as other members that were significantly larger and some that were secondarily carnivorous. The following taxa represent the variety of groups found within the condylarths.

Protungulatum (Early Paleocene, North America). The most primitive known condylarth is *Protungulatum* ("before ungulates"), a rat-sized mammal known primarily from fossil teeth and jaws. Its teeth form an early version of the dental battery characteristic of later condylarths, with long upper and lower canines, slightly

Coryphodon (Middle Eocene, North America) had a stocky build like a tapir or hippopotamus.

pointed premolars, and broad molars with tall cusps. The general shape of the molars made for a good grinding surface to chew plants and possibly insects.

Chriacus (Early Paleocene, Europe). *Chriacus* was a lightly built and smaller condylarth. It was an agile animal, with long legs; a prehensile tail; and a long skull equipped with teeth adapted for eating insects, fruits, and small animals. Measuring a little more than 3 feet (1 m) long, *Chriacus* had plantigrade feet with claws suited for digging and climbing. In lifestyle, *Chriacus* might be likened to a long-legged and swift-moving raccoonlike animal that could climb rapidly through trees and dart along the floors of Paleocene tropical forests.

Mesonyx (Middle Eocene, North America). Among the carnivorous condylarths was *Mesonyx*, a coyote-sized lightweight predator with a low body and deadly canine teeth. Its long snout and oversized head are reminiscent of the wolverine. Carnivorous condylarths evolved from omnivorous ancestors, and their dental batteries were adapted from teeth once suited for eating plants to teeth

Mesonyx (Middle Eocene, North America) was a carnivorous condylarth. It was coyote-sized with a low body and deadly canine teeth.

capable of eating meat. This was done through a modification of the cheek teeth in which the lower molars developed a cutting surface that pressed against the upper molars to pinch and snip meat.

Andrewsarchus (Late Eocene, Mongolia). Considered the largest terrestrial carnivore ever discovered, *Andrewsarchus* was a bizarre combination of hyena and bear. It had an extremely long skull that measured 2.6 feet (83 cm) long and a long snout that may have been handy for a scavenging carnivore. Like *Mesonyx*, *Andrewsarchus* was part of the only group of condylarths to become fully carnivorous. Its teeth included a formidable combination of long, sharp canines and incisors backed by cheek teeth adapted for shearing meat and crushing bone or other hard foods such as shellfish. The feet of *Andrewsarchus* did not have sharp claws but more hooflike nails. Only one definitive specimen of *Andrewsarchus* has been discovered; it consisted primarily of a skull and only fragments of the postcranial skeleton. Extrapolating a possible size for *Andrewsarchus* from the only known fossils, its body length is estimated at up to 18 feet (5.4 m) long.

Fossil collector Roy Chapman Andrews (1884–1960) discovered *Andrewsarchus* during a series of fruitful fossil-hunting expeditions in Mongolia in the 1920s sponsored by the American Museum of Natural History. Although Andrews himself and paleontologist Henry Fairfield Osborn (1857–1935) of the American Museum felt from the start that the gigantic beast was a carnivorous animal, its strange dentition and unusual size led others to conclude that it was a giant, extinct pig. Osborn's study of the skull, published in 1924, showed conclusively that the beast was in fact a meat-eater, and a gigantic one at that. Osborn estimated that *Andrewsarchus* had a "length from the snout to the back of the pelvis of 12 ft. 6.5 in. and a height from the ground to the shoulder or middle of the back of 6 ft. 2 in." In comparing *Andrewsarchus* to living mammals, Osborn added that its cranium was twice the size of that of the Alaskan brown bear, the largest living predatory land mammal, which weighs 1,500 pounds (3,333 kg). Osborn named the spectacular *Andrewsarchus* after its discoverer, Roy Chapman Andrews.

Phenacodus (Early Eocene, Europe). In contrast to some of the other large, slow-moving condylarths was *Phenacodus*, a grazing animal that measured about 5 feet (1.5 m) long and that possibly was close to the ancestry of horses. This sheep-sized mammal had **digitigrade** feet with five toes, but not all of the toes were weight supporting. The first and fifth toes were greatly reduced. This represents an early stage in the consolidation of toes and hooves that is similar to the consolidation that led to the single hoof of the modern horse foot. The limbs of *Phenacodus* were short but flexible—this made it a good runner. The skull, jaws, and teeth of *Phenacodus* were somewhat reduced in proportion to body size. This trait was unlike other large-bodied condylarths, whose skulls and teeth were generally enlarged. The teeth of *Phenacodus* showed advanced specialization for eating vegetation, with low molars equipped with cross ridges for chewing plants instead of angular cusps.

DINOCERATA: DAWN EMPERORS AND GIANT BROWSERS

Dinocerata, the "terrible horns," were the largest of the early Cenozoic browsing mammals, but Dinoceratans are disconnected evolutionarily from modern mammals. The group existed only from about the Late Paleocene to the Middle Eocene, in Asia and North America. In their dentition, these often-large animals had reduced incisors but greatly enlarged canines. They are also noted for their prominent paired horns. Dinoceratans once were thought to be related to the ungulates but now are thought to represent an unrelated lineage. They probably had a lifestyle similar to that of the rhinoceros.

The first scientific description of a dinoceratan was published in 1872 by American paleontologist Joseph Leidy (1823–1891). Leidy was one of three towering figures of nineteenth-century paleontology in America. He was the elder statesman of a trio of overachieving scientists that also included Edward Drinker Cope (1840–1897) of Philadelphia and Othniel Charles Marsh (1831–1899) of New Haven, Connecticut. By 1872, a scientific rivalry had begun to smolder between Cope and Marsh, and the two remained enmeshed in a messy and long-lasting battle over fossils until their deaths. At stake were claims to the fossil vertebrate riches of the American West, to which, for the next 20 years, both men sent expeditions to find and excavate dinosaurs and other spectacular fossil creatures. It was during the early 1870s, however, with the discovery of extinct mammals in the badlands of Wyoming and New Mexico that the seeds of the Cope-Marsh rivalry had begun to grow.

After naming the mammal *Uintatherium* ("beast of the Uintahs") after the Uintah Mountains in Utah, Leidy withdrew from paleontology in 1872. He wanted to avoid getting entangled in the aggressive push for fossil discoveries that Cope and Marsh were underwriting. From 1872 to 1875, prior to their becoming distracted by the even more spectacular discovery of dinosaur fossils, Cope and Marsh raced to scoop each other in print with the announcement of one extinct mammal after another. Many of these mammals were from the Paleocene and Eocene deposits of the American West.

For a time, both Cope and Marsh had fossil collectors working in the same region of Wyoming. The rival teams often dug up different specimens of the same mammals. This only made matters worse because Cope and Marsh each wanted to describe a new creature before his competitor did. The two men worked feverishly, naming and describing fossils as soon as they were dug up. While this might have been good for the rivals' tallies of fossils, it was bad for science. Their analyses often were hurried and incomplete and lacked the benefit of comparative study. Cope and Marsh often were harshly critical of each other's work, and their rivalry spilled over into the pages of newspapers and scientific journals. There, the men slung insults and criticisms at each other in defense of their discoveries.

As far as their rivalry over the dinoceratans was concerned, Cope was a more prolific discoverer of these creatures than Marsh. (See "Think About It: E.D. Cope and the Discovery of Extinct Mammals of the American West.") Marsh was the better organized of the two, however, and he succeeded in publishing a comprehensive, 241-page study of the Dinocerata in 1884. Marsh created the name Dinocerata to describe this group of extinct hoofed Eocene mammals—a name that is still used today to identify them.

In truth, it is no wonder that the dinoceratans fueled such scientific curiosity and envy: They provide some of the most bizarre images we have of prehistoric life.

Prodinoceras (Late Paleocene, China and North America). *Prodinoceras* ("before terrible horns") was an early and smaller member of the dinoceratans, yet it was massively built like those that followed. Known primarily from teeth and skulls from North America and Asia, *Prodinoceras* had the huge upper canines and broadly splayed skull elements behind the eyes that are typical of dinoceratans, but completely lacked the paired horns found on later dinoceratans.

Uintatherium (Middle Eocene, North America). The specimen that inspired the bone war between Cope and Marsh was also the last major contribution to paleontology made by Joseph Leidy of

Philadelphia. The original specimen included many fragments of the jaw, skull, molars, and spectacular tusks of this enormous animal. A more complete picture of *Uintatherium* emerged as further discoveries revealed additional body parts such as the robust limbs, bulky body, and digitigrade feet of this rhinoceros-sized beast. *Uintatherium* had three pairs of bony horns or bumps on its large skull. One pair was at the tip of the snout; another pair was on the skull roof, just before the eyes; a third and even larger pair was on the cap of the skull, behind the eyes. What these horns were used for is a mystery. It is likely, however, that in addition to being helpful in identifying members of the opposite sex, the horns may have come in handy during intraspecies combat between rivals. *Uintatherium* was about 5.5 feet (1.6 m) tall at the shoulder, with a body length of perhaps 11 feet (3.3 m).

Eobasileus (Middle Eocene, North America). One of Cope's first discoveries among the dinoceratans was *Eobasileus*, the "dawn emperor." This was a browser similar to *Uintatherium*, but it was slightly smaller, at about 10 feet (3 m) long. *Eobasileus* had four bony protuberances on its skull instead of the six found on *Uintatherium*, but these were not all apparent to Cope when he first recovered the skull. Cope was recklessly excited about his discovery; he wrote to his father in 1873 that, "In a word, *Eobasileus* is the most extraordinary fossil mammal found in North America."

Cope first believed that *Eobasileus* had a trunk like that of an elephant—an idea for which Marsh harshly criticized him. The similarities of *Eobasileus* to *Uintatherium* in its skull morphology, its limbs, and its general body plan became apparent only after the recovery of additional fossils. Another similarity among the giant dinoceratans is also worth noting. They lacked upper incisors. Both *Eobasileus* and *Uintatherium* had only small incisors in the lower jaw, a trait of modern animals in which the tongue is often long and strong to assist in grasping food.

Gobiatherium (Late Eocene, Mongolia). *Gobiatherium* ("wild beast from Asia"), from Central Asia, was discovered in 1930 by a Mongolian expedition sponsored by the American Museum of Natural History. *Gobiatherium* was one of the last of the dinoceratans. It had a long, low skull that entirely lacked the horns and protuberances seen in North American dinoceratans. *Gobiatherium* also lacked the tusklike canines of *Eobasileus* and *Uintatherium*. It did, however, have a broad, bony tip to its upper jaw, which lacked incisors, as did the jaws of its North American relatives. Another distinguishing feature of *Gobiatherium* was a broadly arched nasal area at the tip of the snout that formed a somewhat cylindrical air passage.

SOUTH AMERICAN HOOFED MAMMALS

There were four uniquely South American groups of ungulates, all of which are now extinct. Lasting from the Early Paleocene to the end of the Pliocene Epoch, 60 million years later, these groups originally were linked to North America but soon evolved on their own as the land bridge connecting the Americas disappeared during the Late Paleocene and Eocene. The origins of these groups might be linked to an ancestral line of condylarths from the Early Paleocene of North America, but that line soon diversified into the South American ungulates' own characteristic groups. South American ungulates evolved independently into forms that were much like those from the Northern Hemisphere; these included moderate- to large-sized herbivores similar to rabbits, horses, rhinoceroses, tapirs, and camels. Other South American ungulates were large, rhinoceros-sized animals. Some of these had trunks, tusklike canine teeth, and impressive batteries of plant-shearing cheek teeth.

Four subgroups of South American ungulates are recognized. Each group probably evolved independently of the others, from separate ancestors from the Northern Hemisphere. The Litopterna included several families of false horses and camel forms. The most varied of all South American ungulates were the Notungulata, which are united by particular specializations of the ear region of the skull and molar dentition. The notungulates ranged in size from rabbitlike forms to large browsers the size of rhinoceroses. The Astrapotheria were moderately large animals with tusklike canines and a body plan somewhat like that of a rhinoceros, but with a

THINK ABOUT IT

E.D. Cope and the Discovery of Extinct Mammals in the American West

Among the most productive, innovative, and provocative of American paleontologists was Edward Drinker Cope. Cope came from a prominent Philadelphia Quaker family and had named his first dinosaur (*Laelaps*, 1866) by the age of 26. By the time of his death, in 1897, Cope had identified and described more than a thousand species of fossil vertebrates from North America—an astounding record of accomplishment that equated to 60 percent of all extinct vertebrates known in his time. Although Cope is most often remembered as the paleontologist who discovered the dinosaurs *Camarasaurus* and *Coelophysis* (among others), some of his most prodigious accomplishments were in the field of fossil mammals. Among these were his discoveries of previously unknown examples of extinct mammal fauna from the Paleocene, Eocene, and Miocene fossil beds of North America.

There is no question that the number of fossil species named by Cope was inflated by his drive to gain priority in publication over his scientific rival, Othniel Charles Marsh of Yale University. Cope never met a fossil that he couldn't name more than once. He eagerly, and mistakenly, assigned nine species names to a single species of the extinct mammal *Loxolophus* (Early Paleocene, New Mexico). This multiple naming often was the result of working with only fragmentary remains, but a more careful practice would have been to leave such partial remains unnamed until further discoveries and comparison to other specimens could demonstrate their true affinity. Cope's lack of nomenclatural caution has resulted in much work for later paleontologists, who have had to sort out his species over the years.

longer neck. The Pyrotheria were massive browsers with tusks and trunks but were unrelated to tapirs or elephants. Key taxa from each of these groups include the following hoofed mammals.

Despite Cope's tendency to name more species than was warranted, many of his mammal discoveries have stood the test of time and have revealed new fossil fauna that were totally unknown before his explorations. Cope's expedition to New Mexico in 1874 was particularly significant: It allowed him to draw connections between mammal fossils of the Eocene of Europe and North America. Cope's successful work in the field—work that he personally supervised—marked a departure from the nearly accidental fossil collecting methods used by Joseph Leidy and other predecessors. In 1937, a student of Cope's, William Berryman Scott, wrote that "Dr. Leidy's material was picked up from the surface of the ground, where the bones had weathered out of the enclosing rock, or matrix, by men who could collect only incidentally, as other work permitted." By comparison, continued Scott, "Professors Cope and Marsh, who had large funds at their disposal, trained a corps of collectors who speedily raised the status of collecting to an art requiring great skill."

Cope claimed to have discovered more than 80 fossil vertebrate species during his 1874 expedition to New Mexico. Even though some of these species later were shown to be redundant, the list of new taxa remains impressive to this day. Among the discoveries from this single season of work were representatives of many archaic eutherian mammal groups—including the creodonts, the pantolestids, the taeniodonts, the condylarths, and the pantodonts—as well as representatives of modern groups that included rodents and early horses (Perissodactyls). Among Cope's finds were extraordinary specimens of the wolverine-sized creodont *Oxyaena* and the large browsing pantodont *Coryphodon*.

Diadiaphorus (Miocene to Pliocene, Argentina). True horses have roots in Asia and became widespread during the middle Cenozoic in North America, Europe, Asia, and Africa—continents that maintained land links that enabled the first horses to become geographically widespread in the Northern Hemisphere. True horses from north of the equator did not make an appearance in South America until about 5 million years ago, when a land bridge was established between North, Central, and South America. This land bridge led to the event named the Great American Interchange. Long before the migration of true horses to South America, however, there were some astounding occurrences of convergent evolution that resulted in the independent evolution on that continent of many horselike mammals.

As in North America, the presence of widespread grassy plains in South America provided ideal conditions for the development of running, herbivorous, hoofed mammals. *Diadiaphorus* was one such horselike creature. It was a litoptern with long, lightweight legs; a long, horselike muzzle; and a dental formula very close to that of primitive horses from North America. Most interestingly, even the hooves of *Diadiaphorus* had evolved in a manner very similar to that of the earliest true horses: *Diadiaphorus* had one enlarged and weight-supporting middle toe, or hoof.

Diadiaphorus's molars were low crowned and not as capable of shredding tough vegetation as the molars of the true horse. This suggests that the diet of *Diadiaphorus* consisted of soft leaves and bushes rather than grasses. *Diadiaphorus* was small; it measured about 4 feet (1.2 m) long. *Diadiaphorus* had an even smaller cousin, *Thoatherium,* that measured a mere 2.5 feet (0.75 m) long.

Macrauchenia (Pleistocene, South America). Another branch of the three-toed litoptern group included the camel-like Macraucheniidae. South American llamas and guanacos are members of the true camels (Tylopoda) from the Northern Hemisphere and are not related to this extinct line of litopterns. The similarity in appearance of llamas and guanacos to the Macraucheniidae might lead the unwary to that conclusion, however. Like the horselike litopterns, the macrauchenids were examples of convergent evolution. They adapted anatomical traits similar to those of hoofed mammals that evolved in similar habitats above the equator.

Macrauchenia ("large camel") was larger than the horselike litopterns; it measured about 10 feet (3 m) long. It was a curious blend of hoofed mammal features, having a long neck like a camel, a long muzzle like a horse, three-toed feet that closely resemble those of hippopotamuses, and an arched back like a llama. The nasal openings were positioned high on the skull, above the eyes—a sure sign that *Macrauchenia* probably had a flexible trunk like a tapir. The teeth of *Macrauchenia* were more highly crowned than those of other litopterns; this is an indication that this animal was better adapted for chewing a wider variety of vegetation. *Macrauchenia* was first described by Charles Darwin (1808–1882) during his famous five-year expedition to South America—the trip that provided much inspiration for the development of his theory of evolution. Darwin certainly was puzzled by the occurrence of macrauchenia and its mosaic of traits seen in living species from Africa.

Notostylops (Eocene, South America). Consisting of more than 100 known fossil taxa, the notoungulates ("southern hoofed animals") were the most diverse group of extinct South American mammals. *Notostylops* was among the earliest notoungulate taxa and was most similar in body plan and lifestyle to a rabbit. Measuring about 1.5 feet (0.75 m) long, *Notostylops* had chisel-like incisors similar to those of a rodent. These teeth did not grow continuously, however, and so were suited for snipping vegetation rather than for gnawing like rats. The canine teeth in *Notostylops* and later notoungulates were greatly reduced. The skull was short, with a broad braincase. The hearing region of *Notostylops* and other notoungulates was enlarged and distinctive; this indicates that these animals had highly acute hearing.

Toxodon (Pleistocene, Argentina). One of the later notoungulates was also the largest. *Toxodon* could be described as rhinoceroslike; it had a spiny ridge over the shoulders and a heavy, hippopotamuslike skull. Its hind legs were longer than its forelimbs; this gave *Toxodon* a forward leaning posture, supported by its flat, or plantigrade, feet. Its cheek teeth were broad and high crowned for chewing plants, and its chisel-like upper incisors were suited for snipping some of the tougher grasses from the plains. These dental adaptations show that later notoungulates had adapted well to a variety of plant sources during the Pleistocene of South America. Darwin was the first scientist to describe Toxodon, and he marveled at its peculiar biology. He declared that it was "perhaps one of the strangest animals ever discovered. . . . How wonderfully are the different orders, at the present time so well separated, blended together in different points of the structure of the *Toxodon!*"

Astrapotherium (Oligocene and Miocene, South America). *Astrapotherium* ("great lightning beast") was an astrapothere, a member of a group that is well represented by several good fossil specimens. *Astrapotherium* represents the typical features of the group. With a body like that of a rhinoceros and a head vaguely resembling that of an elephant, *Astrapotherium* was a low browser. It has been theorized that the animal was a wader like a hippopotamus. The animal had a long body and short skull. Its flat feet were small, and its legs were short. With nasal openings high on the skull, it appears that *Astrapotherium* also had a short trunk. The upper and lower canine teeth formed tusks. The upper tusks were longer than the lower, and the upper canines flared slightly to the sides so that they could shear plants against the shorter, lower canines. As a possibly aquatic browsing animal, *Astrapotherium* may have been similar to a line of extinct rhinoceroses from the Northern Hemisphere—the amynodonts—that had a similar body plan and presumably fed on plants in ponds and lakes.

Pyrotherium (Eocene and Oligocene, South America). *Pyrotherium* ("fire beast") was the most elephantlike South American ungulate and a member of the Pyrotheria. Measuring about 10 feet (3 m) long, *Pyrotherium* had an enormous head, a long body, and plantigrade feet. Its tusks were notably flattened and chisel-like in shape. It had four tusks in the upper jaw and two in the lower, all pointing forward and all continuously growing. Its cheek teeth consisted of massive grinding molars. *Pyrotherium* had nasal opening positioned high on the skull, indicating that the animal probably had a short trunk. *Pyrotherium* was a curious combination of rat and elephant: It had gnawing teeth, a hulking body, and a short trunk. Although the presence of gnawing teeth in a large browsing animal is unusual, such teeth are not unheard of and are in fact a characteristic of some mastodonts, ancestors of true elephants. *Pyrotherium* had a stout, short neck, but the small spines on its backbone suggest that the spine was supported by the weak, long muscles of the back. This paints a picture of a slow-moving browsing animal with limited mobility.

LOST CONNECTIONS, NEW WORLD

The archaic eutherian mammals described in this chapter represent the remarkable early history of mammal evolution. Among the 15 groups and numerous subgroups of extinct mammals described in the chapter were taxa from every continent that arose early in the Paleozoic and persisted, in many cases, for millions of years, successfully adapting to changes in climate and habitat alongside many other groups of mammals that are still among us. The **extinction** of these groups does not always represent a failure to adapt, as in some cases they eventually were replaced by more lucky, opportunistic, and perhaps even better adapted eutherians from other parts of the world.

The success of these extinct eutherians that diversified rapidly after the K-T extinction was largely responsible for establishing the turf of mammals early in the Cenozoic; this led to their dominance during what was named "the Age of Mammals." All extant groups of mammals owe a debt to the evolutionary advances first tested by these conquerors of the forests, tropics, and grasslands of the first half of the Cenozoic Era.

SUMMARY

This chapter reviewed several key groups of extinct eutherian mammals that dominated life on land during the first part of the Cenozoic Era.

1. Early eutherians were well established in North America, Central Asia, and Asia during the latter part of the Mesozoic Era, when the first placental mammals coexisted with the dinosaurs.

2. Archaic eutherians are defined as early placental mammals that survived the K-T transition but became extinct in the early part (i.e., the Paleogene) of the Cenozoic. Some Paleogene groups became extinct without any descendants, whereas other groups are directly related to modern mammal groups.

3. The Taeniodonta included omnivorous tree climbers and diggers that lived in North America from the Early Paleocene to Early Eocene.

4. Pantodonta were some of the first large eutherian browsing herbivores to appear in the Cenozoic; the earliest forms lived in China during the Early Paleocene. They began to appear in North America in the Middle to Late Paleocene as a result of immigration of their Asian counterparts through a land connection that formed during a phase of low global sea level.

5. The Condylarthra were a group of basal hoofed mammals, or ungulates, from the early Cenozoic. They were some of the most common mammals from the Early Paleocene to Late Eocene of North America, Europe, and Asia.

6. The Dinocerata, or "terrible horns," were the largest of the early Cenozoic browsing mammals. They existed from about the Late Paleocene to the Middle Eocene in Asia and North America.

7. There were four uniquely South American groups of ungulates that are all now extinct. They lived from the Early Paleocene to the end of the Pliocene Epoch.

8. South American ungulates evolved from North American ancestors but became geologically and geographically disconnected from the north during the Late Paleocene and Eocene. This caused them to evolve in isolation from relatives in the rest of the world.

9. South American ungulates include the following four groups: the Litopterna (false horse and camel forms); the Notungulata (rabbitlike and hippolike browsers); the Astrapotheria (large, rhinoceroslike browsers with tusks); and the Pyrotheria (large browsers with tusks and trunks).

4

THE ARCHONTA: TREE SHREWS, FLYING LEMURS, BATS, AND PRIMATES

Within the mammal order Archonta are the primates and ancestors of humans, so it is not without special curiosity that this group is introduced. A complete discussion of human origins is a more lengthy matter and is undertaken in two other books in this series, *Primates and Human Ancestors* and *Early Humans*.

Chapter 3 explored extinct eutherians with no obvious evolutionary links to living families of placental mammals. This chapter launches a discussion of the origins and extinct members of extant mammal families and so draws closer to the present day, both in terms of the kinds of mammals that are discussed and the geologic and climatic conditions that govern their existence. This is not to suggest that the discussion of extinct mammals of the later Cenozoic will become monotonous and too familiar. Far from it! In the past 30 million years—the time span that has marked the conquest of modern mammals—Earth has seen major changes to both fauna and living conditions. These changes in turn have led to many diverse evolutionary excursions and so to modern mammals.

Not the least of the factors affecting the evolution of mammals was the introduction of periodic **ice ages** and **interglacial periods** to Earth's natural history. Each of these periods widely affected the adaptation and development of mammals the world over. This chapter and the chapters that follow introduce each major group of living mammals and their extinct ancestors.

The order Archonta is a somewhat loosely knit contingent of mammal groups that appear to be related, although the evolutionary links between them are not fully understood. As late as 1980, the key morphological evidence uniting the Archonta consisted of only a few features—primarily, parts of the ankle bone, similarities of the ear region, and the fact that the male sexual organ was suspended externally with the genital pouch. Since that time, closer examination of the morphology of these animals by anatomist John Wible and paleontologist Michael Novacek and molecular **gene** studies by biologist Ronald Atkins have led scientists to conclude that tree shrews, flying lemurs, and primates have a common ancestor, but that bats diverged from this lineage at an earlier time, thereby forming their own unrelated clan. Although bats are not as closely related to tree shrews, flying lemurs, and primates as once thought, bats are often still grouped with them to form the Archonta and therefore are included in the discussion that follows.

PLESIADAPIFORMES: BASAL ARCHONTANS

The earliest members of the Archonta arose in North America and Europe during the Paleocene and Eocene Epochs. At the base of the primate family tree were the Plesiadapiformes, an extinct group that consisted of the most primitive taxa associated with early archontans. Plesiadapiforms were long-snouted quadrupeds with long tails and squirrel-like limbs equipped with claws for climbing trees. Their jaws and teeth were rodentlike, and they had long incisors. The plesiadapiform dental formula was similar to that of the earliest primates, but the postcranial skeleton of the plesiadapiforms was more like that of flying lemurs. These traits position plesiadapiforms as a possible common ancestor of the earliest primates as well as the flying lemurs.

Purgatorius (Early Paleocene, Montana). Known only from teeth and jaw fragments, the tiny *Purgatorius* had molars that appear to be a primitive form of primate tooth. This small animal was no bigger than a large mouse and weighed little more than 3 ounces (92 grams). It presumably had the body plan of a small rodent.

Plesiadapis (Early Eocene, North America and Europe). The squirrel-like early primate *Plesiadapis* lived between 55 million and 60 million years ago; it lived in forest areas as a tree-climbing quadruped. The dental formula of *Plesiadapis* had a wide gap between the incisors and cheek molars; this gap is a primitive feature and more closely matches the pattern seen in rodent dentition. True lemurs and primates closed this gap and developed a shorter skull with more compressed dentition in the front of the jaw. *Plesiadapis* had upper and lower incisors that were long and that pointed forward like those of a rat. Excellent specimens of *Plesiadapis* include a 4-inch (10 cm) skull that provides evidence for brain capacity, changing development of the inner ear, and improved **olfactory** capacity. Unlike in later primates, the eyes of *Plesiadapis* were still positioned on the sides of the skull. The animal's long, nimble limbs were equipped with flexible wrists and digits with nail-like claws. These features suggest an animal that was quite at home scampering through the trees.

Carpolestes (Late Paleocene and Early Eocene, Wyoming). *Carpolestes* was another cross between a primate and a lemur, with side-facing eyes and grasping hands for tree climbing. A nearly complete fossil skeleton of *Carpolestes*, discovered in 2002, revealed many tantalizing clues that point to a link with the earliest primates. *Carpolestes* was a small, limber climber with a squirrel-sized body that measured 14 inches (36 cm) long. The animal had opposable big toes to allow it to grasp branches firmly, and its teeth, like the teeth of primates, were suited for eating nuts, seeds, and flowers. *Carpolestes* had nails on its toes—a trait of primates—but claws on its other digits. *Carpolestes* was not built for the kind of rapid leaping through trees that primates are known for, however, and, as mentioned, its eyes were not forward pointing. Like *Plesiadapis*, *Carpolestes* was a curious mosaic of old and new features—a **transitional** forerunner of modern archontans with strong hints of an affinity with primates. Paleontologist Jonathan Bloch studied skulls of *Carpolestes* using X-ray computed tomography; he believes that certain features of the internal

Plesiadapis (Early Eocene, North America and Europe) was a squirrel-like early primate that lived in forest areas as a tree-climbing quadruped.

skull anatomy make *Carpolestes* closer to the primates than to other archontans.

Moving on from the early extinct ancestors of archontans, the remainder of this section describes some of the earliest known members of the living groups of tree shrews, flying lemurs, bats, and primates.

SCANDENTIA: TREE SHREWS

These small mammals from Southeast Asia were once classified with the true shrews. More recent analysis places them within the Archonta, however, where they share certain affinities of the skull, large eyes, and large brain size of primates. Within the larger clade, collectively known as the Archonta, the tree shrews have been given their own group, the Scandentia, alongside the primates. Tree shrews have a squirrel-like appearance and today are represented by about 20 species that live in the forests of Southeast Asia.

The fossil record of tree shrews is poor. *Adapisoriculus* (Late Paleocene, France) was discovered in the nineteenth century but is known only from isolated teeth and bone fragments. The affinity of *Adapisoriculus* is uncertain; it could belong to the Insectivora with the true shrews. In 1979, a skull fragment of a possible extinct tree shrew from the Miocene of India was reported and given the name *Palaeotupaia* within the group Scandentia. Other isolated fossil teeth of possible tree shrews have been found in China and Thailand, closer to the domain of living tree shrews. Some of these remains closely resemble those of the extant tree shrew *Tupaia*. It would appear that extinct members of this group were very much like their squirrel-like, long-tailed, big-eared descendants.

DERMOPTERA: FLYING LEMURS

The colugo of Southeast Asia is the only living representative of the Dermoptera, or flying lemurs. The colugo is a tree-living, gliding mammal and is unrelated to true lemurs. The colugo's gliding is done by means of a flap of skin that can be drawn tight and that stretches from hands to feet. A colugo has an additional flap of skin in its tail area, and even the digits of its hands and feet are webbed to improve the total surface area of the wing membranes. Its well-adapted gliding "wings," although incapable of powered flight, are highly effective and give the colugo the distinction of being the best gliding mammal.

The best fossil evidence for extinct flying lemurs was uncovered in the 1990s, when postcranial evidence for two small mammals—*Phenacolemur* (Paleocene to Middle Eocene, North America) and *Ignacius* (Paleocene to Middle Eocene, North America)—indicated that each animal may have had a flying membrane such as that found in modern colugos. These animals also had long, protruding lower incisors and a long snout.

CHIROPTERA: BATS

The only mammals to have developed powered flight are the bats. Unlike the birds before them, the bats achieved this feat by adding a thin membrane to their forelimbs. When vigorously flapped, these membrane-enhanced forelimbs provide the lift that enables bats to fly. A thin, bony frame that consists of four very long fingers supports the forelimb membrane. The umbrellalike wings of bats differ from the wings of pterosaurs, each of whose wing membranes was supported by one long forefinger, and from the wings of birds, whose wings are composed of feathers. Their anatomical means for developing wings aside, the same aerodynamics—the aerodynamics of airfoils—enabled each of these flying creatures to take wing.

The poor eyesight of bats is well documented. In place of good eyesight, bats developed a form of natural radar called echolocation to help them find their way. Bats emit high-frequency audio waves and, with their keen hearing, detect the waves as the sounds bounce back at them. This allows bats to form a three-dimensional sense of the location of objects in the space around them. Because the evolution of this echolocation system involved special modifications to the throat, ears, nose, and brain of the animals, and because all of these modifications can be detected in the empty cavities of fossil skulls, the echolocation system of bats is a key to identifying their fossil ancestors.

There are two kinds of living bats. Small, nocturnal (night-flying) bats make up the majority of species and are known as the

Microchiroptera, or microbats. Larger bats belong to the group Megachiroptera, or megabats. Microbats use echolocation, whereas most megabats do not. Microbats are largely insectivores but also may eat small mammals and fish and suck small amounts of blood from other animals. Megabats are fruit eaters. With more than 1,000 living species, bats make up the second-largest group of extant mammals after rodents.

The earliest evidence of extinct bats is scant. One possible species is known from a tooth found in Late Cretaceous deposits of South America. There then is a gap of more than 10 million years in the fossil record until the first definitive evidence of extinct bats from the Early Eocene of North America. Bats from the Eocene already appear very similar to modern bats, and little is known of the crucial transitional phases in the evolution of bats from small, basal, Mesozoic mammals. Bats are also known from South America, where the earliest known evidence, consisting only of teeth, comes from the Early Eocene of Argentina.

Icaronycteris (Early Eocene, Wyoming). *Icaronycteris* is similar to modern microbats. Among its few primitive features were its short wings and its dental battery, which far exceeded in size and number the dentition seen in modern bats. Whereas modern bats have a claw only on the thumb digit, *Icaronycteris* also had a claw on its first finger. Measuring about 5.5 inches (14 cm) long, *Icaronycteris* had a wingspan of about 15 inches (37 cm). It also had a long tail, a trait not seen in most modern bats. Recent molecular studies of extant bats have been combined with morphological analysis of *Icaronycteris* and other fossil bat specimens to suggest that echolocation evolved in a common ancestor of all bats and then was lost in the megabats.

Palaeochiropteryx (Middle Eocene, Germany). Excellent, fine-grained fossil deposits from the Messel region of Germany provide a rare glimpse of the extinct bat *Palaeochiropteryx*. The deposits in which *Palaeochiropteryx* was found are also known as the Messel oil shales. This Middle Eocene location is known for revealing many fine details of mammal remains—including hair, internal organs, and stomach contents—in addition to the usual bones and teeth. The preservation of specimens of *Palaeochiropteryx* clearly shows traces of wing membranes and body hair. With a wingspan of about 10 inches (25 cm), this bat was designed for low flying. Some Messel bats possibly died while skimming an ancient lake for small fish.

PRIMATES: MONKEYS AND APES

Primates ("of the first") include the biological group made up of all lemurs, monkeys, and apes. More than 200 nonhuman primates live today in tropical regions of the Americas, Africa, and Asia. Primates range widely in size, from the largest gorillas, which weigh 500 pounds (225 kg), to the most diminutive primate, the chipmunk-sized dwarf bush baby, which weighs a mere 2.3 ounces (65 grams). Many primates are social creatures, but there are some that prefer to live alone. Primates also vary in their degree of intelligence; in whether they are most active during the day or at night; and in their dietary preferences, which range from fruits, leaves, and nuts to a more omnivorous diet to which a good proportion of insects and meat have been added.

Primate Traits

Primates are distinguished from other mammals by several traits:

Grasping fingers and toes. All primates have five fingers and toes that are capable of grasping. Primate digits also have flat nails instead of claws; this distinguishes them from other climbing animals such as tree shrews and squirrels. An opposing thumb is another feature of the primate hand. When combined with long fingers that close toward the palm of the hand, this thumb allows a primate to grasp objects such as branches. Opposing thumbs are not unique to primates and are also seen in opossums. Grasping hands are a shared trait that goes back to the earliest primates and is a relict of a mostly tree-dwelling lifestyle.

Generalized dental formula. There is a strong tendency toward omnivory in primates, and their tooth pattern, though **heterodont**, is generalized for the consumption of many food sources. Primate molars are low crowned, with blunt cusps, and primates have a reduced number of incisors and premolars when compared with other mammals. This dental formula made primates highly adaptable to a variety of foods and capable of changing their eating habits quickly based on changes in their environment.

Binocular vision. Unlike in squirrels and other arboreal mammals, whose eyes are situated on the sides of the skull and provide nonoverlapping fields of vision, primate eyes face forward and provide stereoscopic vision. Having two eyes with overlapping fields of vision allows the brain to combine images that are only slightly different in their horizontal projection; the differences provide a sense of depth and dimensionality. This is important to a fast-moving animal because overlapping vision provides more visual data to which the brain can respond. Judging distance is especially important to tree-dwelling animals capable of jumping from branch to branch. The anatomy of the primate skull has several modifications to accommodate **binocular vision**. These include a shorter snout, a flatter face, and a bony ridge on the rear edge of the orbit that forms a protective encasement for the eyes. The latter feature is more pronounced in the more advanced primates, including the great apes and humans.

Enlarged brain. Primates have a reduction in some senses when compared with other mammals—primates' hearing is less acute than that of canines, for example—but other portions of the primate brain have become enlarged over the course of primate evolution. Larger brain capacity provides increased intelligence and improved adaptability—a key factor in the success of primates.

Primates traditionally have been divided into two major groups for classifying purposes. The **prosimians** ("before monkeys") include lower primates with a more squirrel-like body. Traditionally, this group has included the lemurs, the lorises, and the tarsiers. Prosimians are the most primitive primates. The **anthropoids** ("man structure"), or higher primates, traditionally has included monkeys, apes, and humans. Prosimians and anthropoids broke off from a common ancestry about 40 million years ago.

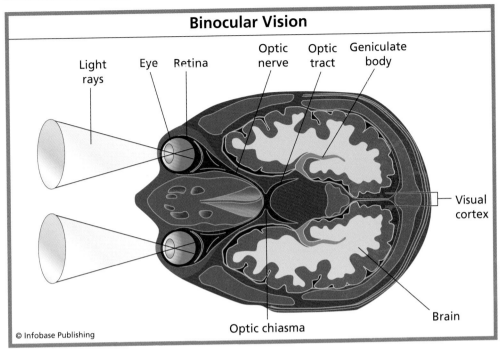

Binocular Vision

Light rays · Eye · Retina · Optic nerve · Optic tract · Geniculate body · Visual cortex · Brain · Optic chiasma

© Infobase Publishing

Binocular vision was a distinguishing feature even of early primates.

Continuing fossil discoveries, morphological analysis, and molecular data led to a rethinking of primate classification during the late 1990s. This rethinking resulted in a revised classification that is widely accepted today. The new view removes the tarsiers from the prosimians and places them in the group formerly known as the anthropoids. In this revised classification, the term *Strepsirhine* is substituted for *prosimians* and the term *Haplorhine* is substituted for *anthropoids*. This revision is based on a more refined definition of each group that combines current knowledge of fossils and molecular analysis. This rethought classification is illustrated in the diagram Primate Clades and Relationships.

The fossil record of primates indicates that Strepsirhines first evolved about 60 million years ago and provided the stock from which the Haplorhines arose, 45 million to 50 million years ago. The precise evolutionary links between Strepsirhines and

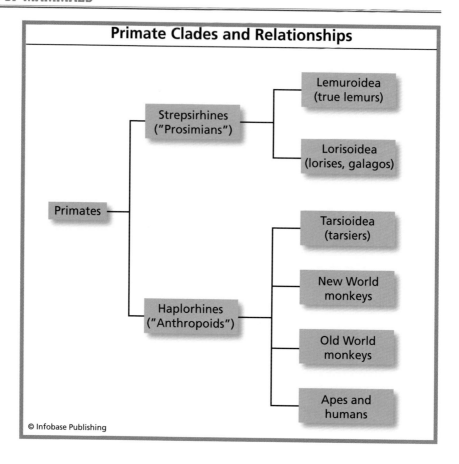

Primate Clades and Relationships

© Infobase Publishing

Haplorhines as well as the geographic origin of primates are not well understood yet from the fossil record and have become a hotly contested issue among paleontologists. The earliest primate fossils are found in northern Africa (Morocco). The scanty Eocene fossil record on that continent has gaps, however, and those gaps make it impossible to test whether primates first diversified in Africa (the "Out of Africa" scenario). As for most groups of placental mammals, paleontologists suspect that primates originated and first evolved in southern Asia during the Late Cretaceous or Paleocene before dispersing into other continents. They probably moved on to other continents—including Europe, Africa, and North America—during the Eocene Epoch.

The Oldest Primates

The earliest examples of fossil primates include several basal Strepsirhines. *Altiatlasius* is the earliest undisputed fossil primate and dates from the Late Paleocene of northern Africa. Even though *Altiatlasius* is known only from 10 isolated molars, these cheek teeth clearly belonged to an early prosimian. Soon after the time of *Altiatlasius,* a diverse assortment of fossil primates appeared across North America, Europe, and Asia. The presence of a fossil primate fauna even during the time of *Altiatlasius* suggests that the true origin of primates might be pushed back to the Early Paleocene or even to the last days of the dinosaurs, about 65 million years ago. Primate paleontologists the world over continue to search Paleocene fossil deposits with the goal of identifying some of the missing pieces of the early primate puzzle.

The case for the geographic origin of primates still hinges on the presence of *Altiatlasius* in northern Africa. The recent discovery of early primate fossils in India and Asia suggests to some paleontologists that North American and European primates had roots in Asia, however, and the search continues, particularly in the Middle Paleocene deposits of southern China, for primate remains that might predate those of Africa.

Basal primates, also known as **euprimates**, have been placed in two groups. The Omomyidae were small tree dwellers. They were similar to tarsiers and are viewed by some as the ancestors of Haplorhines, the higher primates that include apes. Omomyids were restricted to the Eocene Epoch of Europe and Asia. The other major radiation of early primates were the Adapidae, a group of lemurlike forms that existed from the Early Eocene to the Late Miocene and have been found in North America, Europe, Asia, and Africa.

Altiatlasius (Late Paleocene, Morocco). The tiny *Altiatlasius* is known from its molars. It was a small mammal that weighed between 2 and 4 ounces (50 to 100 kg). Although its cheek teeth suggest primatelike dentition close to that of the strepsirhines, no dental formula is known for *Altiatlasius* because only 10 of its teeth were found, and even those were isolated rather than preserved in a jaw fragment showing their positions relative to one another.

Teilhardina (Early Eocene, Europe, North America, and China). The first unequivocal specimens of euprimates are found in Early Eocene deposits of North American and Asian origin. *Teilhardina* was an early omomyid, or tarsierlike primate. *Teilhardina* specimens from North America and Europe consist mostly of isolated teeth, but a recently unearthed Chinese specimen reveals most of the skull, including complete dentition. Of particular interest in this skull are the primitive dentition, the somewhat forward-facing eyes, the enlarged braincase, and the reduced snout. This Chinese specimen of *Teilhardina* has a small skull that measures only about one inch (25 mm) long. The dentition of this specimen suggests that this is the most primitive known member of the omomyids. *Teilhardina*'s having been established in China by the earliest Eocene also suggests that primate origins may be closely linked to Asia rather than to Africa, a theory that needs to be supported by additional fossil evidence predating that of the Moroccan *Altiatlasius*.

Necrolemur (Middle to Late Eocene, western Europe). *Necrolemur* ("grave lemur") was an early omomyid, or ancestral tarsier, that measured about 10 inches (25 cm) long. Its skull had a broad brain cavity, a large ear cavity, and large orbits. These features suggest a nocturnal lifestyle similar to that of living tarsiers. *Necrolemur* was most certainly tree living, and its teeth suggest a diet of insects. As in its cousin *Tetonius* (Middle Eocene, North America), the orbits of *Necrolemur* were somewhat forward facing. This suggests the adaptation of stereoscopic vision. The teeth of these animals were small and pointed, and the creatures also had reduced incisors; this dental formula was ideal for piercing the outer shell of insects. The limb adaptations of *Necrolemur* show an affinity for climbing and for jumping from branch to branch.

Smilodectes (Eocene, North America). *Smilodectes* was a lemurlike adapid and among the most wide-ranging and abundant of the euprimates. *Smilodectes* weighed about 4.6 pounds (2.1 kg). It

Teilhardina (Early Eocene, Europe, North America, and China), one of the first unequivocal examples of euprimates

had a short, lemurlike face and snout. Its braincase indicates that *Smilodectes* had an enlarged visual cortex for improved vision—an indication that this animal was probably active during the daytime. Adapids were generally larger than omomyids. Their long limbs, long bushy tails for balance, grasping hands, and stereoscopic vision would have made adapids agile foragers of fruit and leaves.

Strepsirhines

The Strepsirhines include the living lemurs of Madagascar and the lorises and galagos from tropical Asia and Africa. These small to medium-sized lower primates retain some of the primitive features seen in the plesiadapiforms and the oldest primates. Most have a highly developed sense of smell and keen eyesight. These traits are suggestive of a nocturnal lifestyle in either living or ancestral taxa. The protruding incisors of Strepsirhines form a dental specialization called a tooth comb that is used primarily for grooming. While most of their digits have fingernails, some taxa have special claws on their toes that are used for grooming. Strepsirhines live in trees. The animals have grasping hands and feet but have poorly opposed thumbs. This limits the daredevil nature of their swinging from limb to limb; such daredevil swinging is a characteristic of monkeys and is known as **brachiation**. Strepsirhines move about primarily as quadrupedal animals. Unlike the highly social Haplorhines, Strepsirhines are more solitary creatures and lack the social behavior patterns seen in higher primates.

Strepsirhines have a poor fossil record prior to the Late Pleistocene. Lemurs once roamed widely across Africa, North America, and Europe but are found today only on the island of Madagascar. The lorises have a fossil record that dates back the Eocene of Africa. Today, lorises are found in tropical regions of Africa and Asia.

Extant lemurs are agile, cat-sized creatures that live in trees, so it is surprising to find that there once existed a line of lemurs that were as big as orangutans and gorillas and that lumbered slowly through the trees and along the ground. The geographic isolation of Madagascar from mainland Africa gave lemurs a chance to diversify rapidly and occupy ecological niches filled by monkeys, apes, and other herbivores on the continent of Africa. There also were fewer predators on Madagascar. This gave lemurs the chance to fully exploit their habitat. American biological anthropologist Craig Stanford recently surmised that the story of Madagascar lemurs reveals much about how competition and predation affected the evolutionary potential of early primates. The evolution of traits such as large body size, leaf eating, tree hanging, and having an active daylight lifestyle—characteristics not normally associated with small Strepsirhines—did not occur in other places. Most of these specialized lemurs began to go extinct about 2,000 years ago and eventually succumbed to the arrival of humans and to changes to their habitat because of extensive deforestation.

Megaladapis (Pleistocene to recent, Madagascar). *Megaladapis* was built much differently from living lemurs. Weighing about as much as an adult orangutan, this 165-pound (75 kg) primate was a slow tree climber that moved up and down branches as it foraged for leaves. It had long canine teeth and an oversized, horselike skull that was unlike the skulls seen in any other primates. Its jaws were strong, and its cheek teeth had a narrow shearing edge for grinding leafy vegetation.

Archaeoindris (Pleistocene to recent, Madagascar). *Archaeoindris*, a giant "sloth lemur," was even larger than *Megaladapis*. *Archaeoindris* weighed as much as 440 pounds (200 kg), the mass of a male gorilla. *Archaeoindris* also was a leaf eater, and it could have hung by its elongated hands from tree branches as it slowly browsed for food. Its forelimbs were longer than its hind limbs. This body plan invites comparison to the unrelated tree sloths of Central and South America. With a long body and extended fingers and toes, *Archaeoindris* could have been at home sitting at the base of a tree, slowly pulling branches to its mouth to pluck the leaves.

Haplorhines

The Haplorhines, or anthropoids, were well established in Africa, Europe, and Asia by about 25 million years ago. Their actual origins must have been earlier, and it generally has been agreed that the higher primates were descendants of Eocene Strepsirhines. The section that follows describes the nonhuman members of the Haplorhines. A complete discussion of **hominids**—the group to which humans belong—and the first humans is found in two other books in this series, *Primates and Human Ancestors* and *Early Humans*.

Nonhuman primates of the group Haplorhines include tarsiers, **Old World** monkeys, New World monkeys, apes, and hominids. Living and fossil Haplorhines share a number of traits that separate them from other primates and mammals. The orbit or eye enclosure of the skull forms a protective socket that is closed at the back—a feature lacking in the prosimians and in most other mammals. In contrast to the nostril slits seen in other primates, Haplorhines have rounded nostrils. Haplorhine dentition includes large canines and premolars that closely resemble the Haplorhines' broad, boxy molars. Tarsiers share a suite of anatomical traits that place them somewhat between the prosimians and the anthropoids.

The origin of the Haplorhines—the anthropoids—is as hotly contested by paleontologists as is the overall origin of all primates. While anthropoids are well known from the fossil record by the Oligocene Epoch, their roots are less clear. It is assumed by most paleontologists that Haplorhines arose from the stock of the lower primates, or Strepsirhines.

Origin of the Haplorhines

The earliest forms of higher primates were small, monkeylike animals of a size and with a body plan similar to many of the earlier lower primates. The oldest known fossils believed to be those of an early anthropoid consist of several molar teeth of *Algeripithecus* (Middle Eocene, Algeria). While the occurrence of these fossils in North Africa has argued for an "Out of Africa" origin for the

Haplorhines, the discovery of an equally old and more informative primate specimen from China has complicated this view. The remains of *Eosimias* ("dawn monkey") were discovered by a joint American-Chinese paleontological team between 1994 and 1997. The remains consist of jaw and skull fragments as well as pieces of limb and ankle bones.

Eosimias was a tiny primate, as small as a pygmy marmoset—about 6 inches (15 cm) excluding the tail. Its remains show that many anthropoid traits of the skull and teeth were evolving prior to the attainment of the larger body size associated with most higher primates. The teeth of *Eosimias* were more primitive than those of *Algeripithecus* from North Africa, which suggests that *Eosimias* represented a more ancient branch of anthropoid lineage.

Paleontologist Christopher Beard of the Carnegie Museum of Natural History, the leader of the American half of the team that discovered *Eosimias*, knew that the anatomy of this animal revealed indisputable monkeylike features and represented the earliest definitive evidence for an evolutionary connection between the lower primates and the higher primates. This evolutionary story had great implications for the "Out of Africa" theory of Haplorhine origins. "The fact that *Eosimias* was so much more primitive than roughly contemporary African higher primates," explained Beard, "was potentially one of its most important attributes from a scientific perspective. First, the presence of the most primitive higher primates in China could mean that higher primates actually originated on the Asian landmass, thus bursting the bubble of the 'Out of Africa' hypothesis."

Fragmentary fossils such as those used to ascertain anthropoid origins do not usually lead all paleontologists to the same conclusion. There remain some vocal opponents of an "Out of Asia" origin for Haplorhines, and this saga will continue to unfold as discoveries continue in both China and Africa.

A little later in the fossil record, the existence of early anthropoids is much clearer. One significant source of early Haplorhine fossils is the Fayum Depression, a geologic formation in Egypt.

The fossils from this locality date from the Late Eocene and Early Oligocene. The Fayum Depression is in the Sahara Desert, but the area once was a lush, tropical forest divided by rivers that was home to many kinds of plants and animals. The Fayum Depression is noted for its fossil remains, although most are fragmentary. Among these are several undisputed taxa of extinct anthropoids that include *Oligopithecus*, *Proteopithecus*, and *Catopithecus*. Like *Eosimias*, these primates contained a mosaic of primitive and more derived features of Haplorhines. Also like *Eosimias*, these creatures show that ancestral anthropoids flourished prior to the division of anthropoids into the modern lines of extant primates.

Haplorhine Classification

Living anthropoids are classified into two large groups, the catarrhines ("downward facing noses")—which include Old World monkeys, apes, and hominids—and the platyrrhines ("flat noses"), or New World monkeys. These groups represent an evolutionary divergence that occurred when ancestral primates began to divide into increasingly specialized subgroups.

The catarrhines share a number of traits. These include closely spaced nostrils that point downward and only eight permanent premolars: two upper and two lower on either side of the jaw. Catarrhines are divided further into two additional subgroups, the Cercopithecoidea, or Old World monkeys, and the Hominoidea, which consist of apes and humans. On average, catarrhines are much larger than platyrrhines and have a dental formula that includes long, pointed canine teeth and a gap between the lower front teeth that allows the canines to self-sharpen by rubbing against the lower premolars.

The platyrrhines consist only of what are called New World monkeys. This distinction separates primates from the "old" world of Africa (and, some might say, Asia), where anthropoids originated, from Haplorhines found in the "new" world of the Americas. New World monkeys are distinguished by having widely spaced, round nostrils that point outward and by having a total of 12 permanent premolars: three upper and three lower on either side of the jaw.

Molecular evidence suggests that ancestral anthropoids slowly began to diverge into the catarrhines and the platyrrhines about 40 million years ago. The first fossil evidence of this split includes the appearance of extinct New World monkeys in South America between 30 million and 35 millions years ago. While the New World monkeys have retained a relatively stable body plan and lifestyle since the Oligocene, the catarrhine branch of anthropoids has diverged further into several different groups. These include the colobines, the gibbons, the orangutans, the gorillas, the chimpanzees, and humans.

Tarsiers

The tiny tarsier is at the center of the debate over the origin of Haplorhine primates and the line of apes that leads to the evolution of humans. There is little doubt that the most humanlike of Haplorhines—the hominids—evolved in Africa beginning around 10 million years ago. The more ancient roots of human ancestors reach back, however, to the nonhuman Haplorhines and to tarsiers in particular because although tarsiers share many traits with the euprimate omomyids, tarsiers have characteristically large eyes, ankle bones, and other specialized skeletal features that are more closely allied to anthropoids. Tarsiers are a kind of biological bridge between the lower primates and the higher primates. For these reasons, tarsiers are grouped with the Haplorhines in this discussion, although a more traditional view might still place them in the Strepsirhines.

Shoshonius (Early Eocene, Wyoming). This ancient tarsier is known from six fossil skulls first described in 1991. The discovery of *Shoshonius* was instrumental in raising questions about the affinity of tarsiers in the lineage of anthropoids. The fine preservation of these specimens revealed details not previously seen in early primate fossils. *Shoshonius* had enlarged eye sockets and details of the ear region of the cranium that reflected similar traits found in living tarsiers.

The ear canals of mammal skulls are particularly informative when scientists are trying to classify fossil mammals because details of the ear region vary distinctly from taxon to taxon and provide clues to derived traits that develop as new species evolve.

Shoshonius proved to be more modern than expected for a 50 million-year-old primate and has since been considered one of the earliest crossovers from the lower primates to the line of higher primates that eventually led to the anthropoids. In addition to its large eyes, *Shoshonius* had a reduced snout and a quadrupedal posture, with elongated leg and foot bones for climbing and leaping in trees. Its closely packed teeth were sharply cusped, indicating a diet of insects.

Old World Monkeys

The broadest and most primitive group of primates is the Cercopithecoidea, or Old World monkeys. The Old World monkeys also are the most diverse group; members have adapted not only to the tropical climates of Africa and Asia but also to more moderate habitats in the Mediterranean and Japan. Living primates of this group include baboons, macaques, and the colobus monkey, among others. Old World monkeys are quadrupedal and use their tails for balance. Cercopithecoids have a unique, four-cusped, boxy molar tooth design that is not seen in other anthropoids.

Old World monkeys differ significantly from hominoids (apes and humans) in several ways. Monkeys in general have a long back, a narrow chest, and a range of shoulder motion that is more restricted than that of the hominoids. Monkeys have tails, often prehensile in nature, whereas hominoids do not. These anatomical features have suited Old World monkeys well for a life in the trees as functional quadrupeds that can hang and swing from branches or run on the ground on all fours.

Apidium (Late Eocene, Egypt). This early relative of the Old World monkeys marked a divergence in the evolution of New World monkeys from the cercopithecoids. *Apidium* was a moderately sized monkey with long limbs for running and leaping between branches.

Weighing about 2.2 pounds (1 kg), *Apidium* probably lived the lifestyle of the living squirrel monkey. Its teeth reveal that it ate fruits and seeds. It moved about on all fours, running and leaping across tree branches in northern Africa. Unlike later Old World monkeys, *Apidium* had three premolars instead of two. This strongly suggests that it evolved at the base of the Old World monkey family tree, prior to the split between the New and Old World lineages.

Aegyptopithecus (Early Oligocene, Egypt). *Aegyptopithecus* is another early monkey from the Early Oligocene of Egypt. Unlike *Apidium*, *Aegyptopithecus* had a dental formula like that of the Old World monkeys, with two premolars instead of three. *Aegyptopithecus* represented an increase in the body size of primates; it probably had an average body weight of about 15 pounds (6.8 kg). This means that this anthropoid was as big as a large house cat. The canine teeth were longer in some specimens and most likely belonged to males; this provides an early glimpse of a **sexually dimorphic** feature still recognized in living primates. Also known as the "dawn ape," *Aegyptopithecus* had traits that are ancestral to Old World monkeys as well as to apes, thereby making it an important link in the ancestry of anthropoids.

Victoriapithecus (Middle Miocene, Kenya). Whereas *Apidium* and *Aegyptopithecus* represent early stages in the formation of the group known as the Old World monkeys, *Victoriapithecus* represents the group's oldest undisputed fossil member. *Victoriapithecus* serves as a link between the much older *Aegyptopithecus* and later Old World monkeys. Weighing between 7 and 15 pounds (3 to 6.8 kg), *Victoriapithecus* was a quadrupedal monkey that probably was as much at home running along tree branches as it was running on the ground. As such, it was one of the earliest anthropoids to shift from a lifestyle that was mostly in the trees to one that was equally at home on the ground. Its jaws include the four-cusped molars that are characteristic of the cercopithecids. Its orbits were completely encased in bone, giving its foreskull a rather apelike appearance.

(continues on page 96)

THINK ABOUT IT

Lasting Impressions: The Exquisite Fossils of Messel and Fayum

Usually, our windows to the prehistoric past are open hardly more than a crack. Occasionally, however, a window opens wide to disclose a wealth of fossil evidence for a particular place and time. Two such windows to the past are found in the Messel oil shales of Germany and the fossils of the Fayum Depression, a geologic formation in Egypt.

The youngest of these two windows is the Fayum site, which dates from the border of the Eocene and Oligocene, between 33 million and 36 million years ago. The Fayum Depression contains many early mammal fossils. Now a desert, the Fayum environment was once a tropical coastal plain with tall trees and zigzagging streams—a warm swamp with seasonal flooding. Today, the remains of mangroves and other plants are found among the remains of many taxa of extinct animals. Other portions of the extensive formation include marine sediments that contain fossils of the early whale *Basilosaurus*. The ancient environment favored the rapid sinking and burial of dead or entrapped animals. This accident of preservational bias benefits paleontologists by revealing the largely intact, often **articulated**, partial and complete remains of extinct animals.

More than 30 different groups of extinct mammals and other vertebrates have been discovered at Fayum, and they provide a remarkably complete picture of the ecology of that long-ago time. Among the creatures found at Fayum are the rhinoceros-sized *Arsinotherium*, with its large, prominent nasal horns; sea cows; credonts; early proboscids; the first marsupial known from Africa; primitive hoofed mammals; bats; birds; rodents; and a host of others. Among the most valued and impressive Fayum fossils are those of primates and early anthropoids.

Fayum contains the earliest unambiguous anthropoid fossils found anywhere. Of the 14 genera of primates found at Fayum, 10 clearly are related to monkeys and apes. One of the best represented of these early primates is *Aegyptopithecus*, a 15-pound (6.8 kg), short-limbed, slow-moving tree climber about the size of a howler monkey. The skull and jaws of *Aegyptopithecus* serve as an important link between Eocene primates and the Miocene hominoids that came later. Fayum is one of the best sources of fossils for arboreal primates; these animals presumably fell from trees, drowned, and were buried whole or in part in the murky stream and lake sediments.

Whereas the Fayum formation provides one of the best records of early primate evolution, the Messel oil shales site near Frankfurt, Germany, provides exquisitely preserved remains of Middle Eocene mammals, birds, reptiles, fish, insects, and plants from about 50 million years ago. Many of the small creatures preserved at Messel are found whole and often reveal remarkable detail about hair, internal organs, and even the contents of their stomachs. Messel was once an area of small lakes surrounded by subtropical forests. The source of the fossils is a **sedimentary** rock known as oil shale. This type of sedimentary rock is formed at the bed of a still lake environment, where oxygen circulation is limited and where whatever sinks to the bottom gets buried by successive layers of sediment and dying vegetation. The resulting fossils are fine grained and spectacular in every detail.

Among the Messel fossils are crocodiles, turtles, toads, frogs, salamanders, snakes, birds, lizards, bats, and mammals. Although mammals make up only about 3 percent of the fossil fauna found at Messel, they constitute one of the best fossil records of an important span in the early evolution and radiation of mammals. Within the Messel shales are no less than 13 different groups of mammals. These include early insect eaters; opossums; rodents; hoofed mammals (artiodactyls and perissodactyls); an extinct horse ancestor (*Propalaeotherium*); condylarths; and bats. *Leptictidium*, a long-snouted early insectivore, has been found on several occasions with evidence of its last meal, including insect shells, bones of small reptiles and mammals, and pieces of plants.

As if to taunt paleontologists, the clarity of some Messel specimens often can be a source of great controversy as to their true affinities within the family of mammals. The ant-eating mammal *Eurotamandua* found at Messel is clearly similar to true South American anteaters in almost every way, yet it would have been geographically impossible for the two lines to have been associated with each other. Their similarities are due, apparently, to convergent evolution.

(continued from page 93)

Mesopithecus (Late Miocene to Late Pliocene, Greece, Italy, Iran, and Afghanistan). *Mesopithecus*, the "middle ape," is another extinct taxon of Old World monkey. Measuring about 4 feet (1.3 m) long and about 14 inches (35 cm) at the shoulders when walking on all fours, *Mesopithecus* had a long body, a tail, and elongated hands adapted for terrestrial locomotion. Like modern colobines, it was well adapted for life on the ground and lived in open woodland habitats where running would be advantageous. It may be the ancestor of the modern langur monkey that still is found in India today. The langur is a type of colobine. *Mesopithecus* had small incisors and cheek teeth and probably was a leaf eater.

New World Monkeys

The platyrrhines, or New World monkeys, include several closely related families of monkeys from Central and South America. The group includes capuchins, squirrel monkeys, tamarins, marmosets, spider monkeys, howler monkeys, and several others. Most of these taxa are small, arboreal primates that are exclusively herbivorous or supplement their diet with insects.

New World monkeys had a common ancestor with the Old World monkeys; the roots of both groups lie with the euprimates described above. New World monkeys split from the Old World monkeys about 35 million years ago. The earliest New World monkey fossils are found in the Late Oligocene of Bolivia. Just how the platyrrhines got to South America is not entirely known. The prevailing theory is that they rafted—rode fallen trees or other debris—and island hopped from Africa to South America during a time span when sea levels dropped. This drop exposed ocean ridges as islands that provided a pathway.

Branisella (Late Oligocene, Bolivia). *Branisella* is the earliest known specimen of New World monkey. This small primate weighed about 2.2 pounds (1 kg). Remains of *Branisella* are fragmentary but reveal important clues about the animal's teeth and jaws. Jaw fragments described in 1996 showed that the dentition of *Branisella* was very similar to that of early anthropoids from the Late Eocene deposits in Fayum, Egypt. This supports the idea that the first New World monkeys had origins on the African continent.

Protopithecus (Pleistocene, Brazil). Picture a spider monkey that weighs 55 pounds (25 kg) yet still is capable of swinging freely from branch to branch and you have an idea of the unprecedented size of *Protopithecus*. When it was described in 1838, based only on fragmentary limb remains, this taxon was one of the first fossil primates ever to be named. The discovery of a complete skeleton in the 1990s revealed the true identity of this primate, the largest New World monkey known thus far. *Protopithecus* had long arms well suited for suspending itself from branches and swinging from tree to tree. The skull was large and rounded, with a protruding upper jaw outlined by large canines. The animal's large, robust size shows that platyrrhine primates were most likely a significant component of the ecology of the Pleistocene paleoenvironment of South America. *Protopithecus* lived in a habitat that combined prominent forest cover with grazing lands sufficient for such browsing herbivores as *Toxodon*, fossils of which have also been found in the area.

Apes (Hominoidea)

With the passing of the Oligocene Epoch, the face of the Earth and its habitats were transformed dramatically from the warm, tropical Eocene world that had spawned the early radiation of primates. The continents drifted farther apart. North America became isolated from Europe, and India, once a drifting island, fused with Asia. Africa became cleanly isolated from most of Eurasia. The collision of tectonic plates caused massive rift faulting in Eurasia, Africa, and Antarctica. This rift faulting created mountains, valleys, and sweeping habitat changes. A phenomenon called the African superswell, which began during the Early Oligocene, formed mountainous rifts from the Arabian Peninsula down through most of eastern Africa. A cooling trend that largely affected the Northern Hemisphere made the once-tropical habitats of North America, Europe, and Asia inhospitable for primates, which subsequently disappeared from many areas above the equator.

By the beginning of the Miocene, primate populations were largely isolated on their respective continents. The Old World monkeys and early anthropoids were in Africa, India, Southeast Asia, and Japan, and the New World monkeys were in South and Central America. This concentration of primate populations led to an explosion of evolutionary trends in Africa. The main product of this evolutionary explosion was the rapid rise of the apes and the eventual appearance of humans.

The Hominoidea, or apes, today include the gorillas and chimpanzees from Africa, the gibbons and orangutans from Asia, and humans. The hub of ape evolution was eastern Africa, along the area where the Great Rift Valley was developing. The earliest fossils of true apes are known from Kenya, Namibia, Uganda, and Ethiopia. Apes of the Miocene formed a much more diverse group than today. Miocene apes were forest dwellers and primarily fruit eaters, and they lived in an environment that was largely forested. Whereas living nonhuman apes are restricted to just four taxa, Miocene apes are known from literally dozens of taxa. The earliest apes typically had bodies similar to those of monkeys; however, their skulls and dental formula were apelike.

With continued upheaval of the African continent, the climate and habitats of eastern Africa changed dramatically beginning in the Middle Miocene. Africa and Europe joined once again, creating a migration path northward. The African environment became drier, grassier, and less wooded. This was a negative development for apes, which subsisted primarily on forest fruits. As the forests dwindled and fruit became less available, leaf-eating Old World monkeys arose to become the most populous primates. This change in prominence most likely occurred because leaves were more abundant than fruit and were easier for the smaller, agile monkeys to forage.

Apes declined in numbers but made other adaptive adjustments. It was during the Middle Miocene that the roots of modern apes took hold. Some ape forms migrated to the north to populate Europe and Asia. By the Late Miocene, human ancestors had diverged from the

Proconsul (Early Miocene, Africa)

lineages of gorillas and chimpanzees. The following are representative taxa of extinct nonhuman apes.

Proconsul (Early Miocene, Africa). The most abundant group of hominoids from the Early Miocene belonged to the taxon *Proconsul* ("before Consul"). The original specimen consisted only of a jaw and was recognized as having affinities with apes when it was named, in 1933. The specimen was named for Consul, a popular performing chimpanzee in Europe. The fossil was recognized as an important clue to early fossil apes, about which little was known in the 1930s.

A 1947 expedition to the Lake Victoria area of Kenya, mounted by anthropologists Louis Leakey (1903–1972) and his wife Mary

Leakey (1913–1996), resulted in the spectacular find, by Mary Leakey, of a fairly complete specimen of *Proconsul*. The discovery and study of *Proconsul* represented an important contribution to the study of hominoid and even human evolution. Louis Leakey said of *Proconsul* that it seemed to be "neither an ancestral ape, nor yet an ancestor of man, but a side branch with characteristics of both stocks." This rational assessment has more or less stood the test of time, even as many more Miocene hominoids have been discovered.

Proconsul is known from three species that range in weight from about 24 to about 190 pounds (10.9 to 86.7 kg). With a long back and slender limbs, the *Proconsul* body was much more like that of a monkey than a modern ape, although *Proconsul* lacked a tail. Its skull and teeth were more apelike, with hominoid dentition. It probably lived in trees and was adept at swinging from branch to branch.

Proconsul once was considered the last common ancestor held by apes and Old World monkeys, but that distinction now may go to another Miocene hominoid, *Morotopithecus* (Early Miocene, Uganda). *Morotopithecus* includes an even more radical mosaic of monkeylike and apelike features than *Proconsul*. Specifically, the dentition of *Morotopithecus* was less derived and more like that of monkeys than apes, and the postcranial skeleton of *Morotopithecus* featured a shorter, stiffer back and a shoulder girdle that was better adapted for apelike arm swinging than for brachiation.

Afropithecus (Middle Miocene, Africa). Weighing an average of 110 pounds (50 kg), *Afropithecus* was a moderately large hominoid. It is known from fragments of its skull, jaw, and skeleton. *Afropithecus* had a long, narrow snout; relatively small eyes; and robust, tusklike canine teeth. The protruding upper incisors were wide and flat and appear to have worked in concert with the large canines to gather and grind hard seeds and nuts. *Afropithecus* is considered close to the origins of modern hominoids.

Sivapithecus (Late Miocene, Africa, Europe, and Asia). *Sivapithecus* represents a line of Miocene hominoids that radiated widely after the land bridge between Africa and Eurasia was reestablished during the Middle Miocene. *Sivapithecus* was discovered first in India and Pakistan, but examples since have been found in such widely separated regions as Turkey, Kenya, and China. The facial and dental traits of *Sivapithecus* were similar to those of the living orangutan, and it is likely that *Sivapithecus* was ancestral to the modern lineage of Asian great apes. Its body was not very orangutanlike, however, and it had grasping feet more like those of the chimpanzee. *Sivapithecus* measured about 5 feet (1.5 m) tall. The thick enamel of its teeth indicates that *Sivapithecus* fed largely on hard foods such as nuts and seeds.

Dryopithecus (Middle to Late Miocene, Africa, Europe, and Asia). One line of European hominoids is represented by *Dryopithecus*, part of a group that may have included the common ancestor of the modern gibbons and great apes (chimpanzees and gorillas). *Dryopithecus*, which had typically hominoid molars, was a small, tree-climbing animal adapted to eating fruit. *Dryopithecus* measured about 24 inches (60 cm) long. It had a body more like that of a chimpanzee than that of a monkey, so although *Dryopithecus* was most certainly a good climber, it was also well adapted for moving about on the ground. This adaptation would have been important in the Late Miocene world as grasslands and open expanses of land became more common.

Pierolapithecus (Middle Miocene, Spain). *Pierolapithecus* was first described by a team of Spanish paleontologists in 2004. It is one of the best candidates for a group that consists of the last common ancestors of the modern great apes, which include chimpanzees, gorillas, and humans. *Pierolapithecus* existed at just about the time that apes diverged from other hominoids. An excellent specimen of *Pierolapithecus* that consists of skull parts, hands, feet, vertebrae, and other fragments appears to represent a single adult male that may have weighed about 75 pounds (34 kg). Its flat rib cage, stiff lower spine, and flexible wrists and shoulder girdle made it adaptable for tree climbing as well as for so-called knuckle walking while on the ground.

Gigantopithecus (Late Miocene to Pleistocene, China, India, and Pakistan). The largest of all known apes was *Gigantopithecus*, a monstrous primate that probably was most like an orangutan. It is known only from fragmentary fossils that include jaws and teeth. When these fragmentary remains are scaled up to predict body proportions, some estimates make *Gigantopithecus* as much as 10 feet (3 m) tall, with a weight of 1,200 pounds (545 kg). As big as it was, *Gigantopithecus* probably subsisted on such tough vegetation as bamboo, nuts, and seeds as well as on fruit. The last of the line of these giant apes died out only about 300,000 years ago, a time that they shared with early humans.

A WORLD OF CHANGES

The evolution of early primates took place in the midst of dramatic changes in geologic and climatic conditions that significantly affected life on Earth. Even as primates rose and diversified, their world was transformed. It turned from a warm, tropical jungle to a dry, temperate woodland. With this change came modifications to the plants on which most primates fed. Earth's **flora** shifted from the soft, moist vegetation found in tropical forests to the hard nuts, seeds, leaves, and fruits of drier forests.

Early primates were successful largely because they were able to adapt quickly to these environmental changes. Survival of the primates hinged on several important anatomical changes; these included stereoscopic vision, specialized dental formulas, and the modifications to limb structure that empowered their mobility, not only in the trees but also on the ground.

The modification of the primate jaw was a key factor in primate success. As their upper and lower jaws and related musculature became stronger, primates were able to chew tougher foods. This widened their dietary choices. Biological anthropologist Craig Stanford takes the improvement of primate jaws a step further when he suggests that stronger jaws led to the ingestion of more food and to the gradual development of larger body size.

The improvement of the primate jaw seems linked to the changing climate of the Miocene. As a cooling trend converted the tropical forests of eastern Africa and southern Asia into grasslands dotted with woodland patches, primates were well equipped to keep pace with the changes. The environmental stresses present in the Late Miocene were an important influence on the emergence of the great apes from the larger body of generalized anthropoids.

Fossil and living humans belong to the hominoid subgroup called hominids. Human ancestors diverged from other apes—the chimpanzees and gorillas—during the Late Miocene, about 8 million years ago. The reasons for this divergence and the development of the human species are explored in another book in this series, *Early Humans*.

SUMMARY

This chapter launched a discussion of the origins and descriptions of extinct members of extant mammal families.

1. The Archonta is a somewhat loosely knit contingent of mammal groups that appear to be related, although the evolutionary links between them are not fully understood.
2. The earliest members of the Archonta arose in North America and Europe during the Paleocene and Eocene Epochs and are known as Plesiadapiformes. They were long-snouted quadrupeds with long tails and squirrel-like limbs equipped with claws for climbing trees.
3. The Scandentia, or tree shrews, are small mammals, today restricted to Southeast Asia, that share certain affinities of the skull, large eyes, and large brain size of primates. They arose during the Late Paleocene of Europe.
4. The colugo of Southeast Asia is the only living representative of the Dermoptera, or flying lemurs. The colugo is a tree-living, gliding mammal and is unrelated to true lemurs. The ancestors of the colugo arose from the Paleocene to Middle Eocene Epochs of North America.

5. The Chiroptera, or bats, are the only mammals to have developed powered flight. Bats from the Eocene already appear very similar to modern bats, and little is known of the crucial transitional phases in the evolution of bats from small, basal, Mesozoic mammals.

6. Primates ("of the first") include the biological group composed of all lemurs, monkeys, and apes.

7. Common traits of primates include grasping fingers and toes, a generalized dental formula for omnivorous eating, binocular vision, and an enlarged brain.

8. Primates traditionally have been divided into two major groups for purposes of classification. The prosimians ("before monkeys") include lower primates with a more squirrel-like body; today this group includes only the lemurs, lorises, and tarsiers. The anthropoids ("man structure"), or higher primates, include monkeys, apes, and humans.

9. Prosimians and anthropoids broke off from a common ancestry about 50 million years ago.

5

Hoofed Mammals: The Ungulata

One-half of all known mammalian herbivores are hoofed and have roots that go back to the condylarths of the Early Paleocene. Hoofed mammals are familiar today in the forms of horses, tapirs, rhinoceroses, pigs, camels, cattle, and many other taxa. Extinct forms were equally diverse and included the largest of all known land animals, *Paraceratherium,* from the Oligocene of Central Asia and Pakistan. Curiously, the whales and dolphins (order Cetacea) are ungulates taxonomically and are closely related to artiodactyls, having returned secondarily to a marine environment after having begun as hoofed mammals. This chapter explores the wide range of extinct hoofed mammals and the widely divergent adaptations that led to their success in many habitats, both terrestrial and aquatic.

CLASSIFICATION OF THE HOOFED MAMMALS

Hoofed mammals, or ungulates, have evolved independently on two separate occasions. The extinct hoofed mammals that were exclusive to South America were discussed in Chapter 3. The majority of hoofed mammals that persist today have roots in the Northern Hemisphere, where they diversified quickly into many herbivorous niches.

The Ungulata ("hoofed beasts") are divided into three subgroups. The **Artiodactyla** include the even-toed hoofed mammals such as pigs, camels, deer, giraffes, cattle, goats, antelopes, and many others. The **Perissodactyla** include the odd-toed hoofed mammals such as tapirs, rhinoceroses, and horses. The subgroup **Cetartiodactyla** was created only recently to include whales and artiodactyls and is based on studies (both molecular and morphological) showing that cetaceans evolved from terrestrial, artiodactyl ancestors.

The ungulates listed above originated in the late Paleocene of Asia and eventually migrated south to Africa and South America. There are no hoofed mammals native to Australia.

The key to classifying the artiodactyls and perissodactyls naturally begins with the nature of their hooves. Because the earliest mammals had five toes, an initial assumption that can be made about hoofed mammals is that they radically modified and reduced the number, shape, and composition of their toes because of **natural selection**. Among the ancestors of hoofed mammals were taxa that must have possessed some reduction in the toes because of genetic mutations. These individuals survived and passed along this genetic trait to their offspring, thus continuing a reduction in digits that took place over millions of years.

Over time, the limb bones and foot bones elongated, and these animals began to walk and run on their toes in a digitigrade fashion. The continuing reduction of their toes into hooves provided a sturdier foot and better traction, thus improving the chance for survival of runners and browsers alike. These modifications of the foot were accompanied by changes to the ankles and by fusion of the limb bones of the lower leg that are usually paired in other mammals.

Artiodactyls have either two or four toes. In some taxa, the outermost digits (digits 1 and 4) have been greatly reduced and are no longer weight bearing. This adaptation can be seen in fossil taxa as well. Perissodactyls have one, three, or five toes; in some taxa, the middle toe generally bears most of the weight of the animal. In both artiodactyls and perissodactyls, the weight-bearing toes often become enlarged, forming the hoof.

Ungulates represent a wide range of adaptations to habitats and lifestyles. In addition to their feet and limbs, some common traits of some hoofed mammal taxa include the following:

Dentition. Ungulates commonly have robust cheek teeth for grinding vegetation. In modern taxa, these teeth include broad molars with high crowns; the earliest ungulates had rather generalized, low-crowned molars, however. Most artiodactyls lack upper incisors. Canines and the front-most premolars generally are reduced in ungulates.

Digestive Tract. To digest the tough cellulose found in grasses and other fibrous vegetation, hoofed mammals developed a multichambered gut wherein food was passed and redigested through several stages of processing. These chambers within the digestive tract also house symbiotic microorganisms that convert the cellulose and lignin of plant cell walls into digestible nutrient. This highly efficient system for extracting nutrients from seemingly substandard food sources such as grasses and other foliage allowed hoofed mammals to become the dominant herbivores in grasslands and open plains. The name **ruminant** is given to modern two-toed hoofed mammals such as cows and deer that redigest their food in this manner. After giving a mouthful of food an initial chewing, a ruminant swallows it, and it passes into the first chamber of the stomach. There it is partially digested. After that partial digestion, the food is returned to the mouth, chewed a second time, and then swallowed for good. The only artiodactyls that do not chew their "cud" (as the partially digested food is called) are hippopotamuses and pigs.

Horns and Adornments. Some hoofed mammals developed horns for defense, intraspecies competition, and sexual display. Skull outgrowths of hoofed mammals are composed of a variety of materials. These outgrowths include bony antlers that can be shed, as in deer; permanent bony horns with a core surrounded by a sheath, as in cows; skin-covered bony bumps called ossicones, as in giraffes; and horns composed of an outgrowth of finely matted hair, as in rhinoceroses.

The earliest ungulates were small, hornless mammals that lived in forests. They diversified more rapidly with changing climates during the Paleogene, but several dominant groups of extant ungulates appeared with the coming of drier grasslands during the Miocene Epoch.

ARTIODACTYLA: PIGS, HIPPOS, CAMELS AND THEIR ANCESTORS

Today, artiodactyl taxa outnumber perissodactyl taxa by about thirteen to one. Fossil taxa are equally varied, having branched into as many as 20 groups, 10 of which are still living.

Diacodexis (Early Eocene, Eurasia and North America). *Diacodexis* was an early artiodactyl. At about 19 inches (50 cm) long, it was about the size of a cat. Its teeth were low crowned and adapted for eating fruit, leaves, and seeds. Its limbs were long and featured an important clue to its position at the root of the artiodactyl family tree: an ankle showing a small, compact bone (astragalus) that was articulated to allow flex between the lower leg bones and the ankle. *Diacodexis* had five digits on each forefoot and four on each hind foot, but it had already developed small hooves on digits 3 and 4 of each. These small hooves bore most of the animal's weight. Its digitigrade posture and long legs probably made *Diacodexis* a swift runner and leaper.

Entelodon (Middle Eocene to Middle Miocene, China, North America, and Europe). *Entelodon* and its relatives were truly the horror hogs of the Eocene and Miocene. This representative of the extinct pigs was a large, intimidating omnivore that may have eaten plants but also scavenged for meat. *Entelodon* had a mouth with an alarming gape and bone-crushing, conical teeth. Tooth wear suggests that these animals often fed on the flesh and bones of other animals. These distant ancestors of modern pigs were much larger than modern pigs and built quite differently. The *Entelodon* skull was monstrous. It was more than 3 feet (1 m) long, with jaws bearing large upper and lower canines that the animal used to uproot plants and rummage through carcasses. The skull had long, bony bumps on the cheeks, just below the eye sockets. These bumps probably protected the animal as it defended itself or jousted with other members of its species.

Entelodon had long, somewhat slender legs that were shorter on the bottom than on top. This limited the speed at which this massive animal could run. As in later ungulates, however, *Entelodon*'s lower leg bones had become fused, and its digits were reduced to two weight-bearing hooves. With a shoulder height of about 4.5 feet (1.4 m) and a length that sometimes reached 10 feet (3 m), *Entelodon* was one of the largest mammals in its world and nearly immune from attack. Its North American cousins included *Archaeotherium* (Oligocene, South Dakota) and *Dinohyus* (Early Miocene, North Dakota), the "terrible pig."

Hippopotamus (Middle Miocene to present, Africa, Asia, and Europe). *Hippopotamus* has a short and fragmentary fossil history, but today's hippo is quite similar to its ancestors that lived in the Pleistocene. Modern hippos fall into two taxa, both from Africa. These are the familiar, semiaquatic hippopotamus and its smaller cousin, the pygmy hippo, which leads a life browsing through forest vegetation. Fossil evidence for each has been found from the Miocene.

The larger taxa of extinct hippos differed from modern semi-aquatic species in that the extinct hippos' eyes protruded slightly above the face, out of the sockets, as if to increase their peripheral vision or perhaps to lift their eyes out of the water while the rest of the head was submerged. The feet of these extinct hippos were hooved but were more like those of the terrestrial pygmy hippo. This suggests that earlier hippos lived their lives more equally on land and in the water. It is worth noting that molecular and genomic data consistently place hippos as the closest living relatives of whales and dolphins. This result is not clearly corroborated by fossil data so far.

Synthetoceras (Middle Oligocene to Early Pliocene, North America). *Synthetoceras* was from a line of early, deerlike browsers that actually were more closely related to camels than to modern deer. These early ancestors of the camels occupied the warm, southern forests of North America for more than 30 million years. Beginning as smaller taxa no more than about 3.3 feet (1 m) long, these tylopods (extant camels and closely related extinct taxa) ate soft vegetation and developed two-toed hooves over the course of their evolution. One characteristic of the early camels was a variety of horns, bumps, and antlers. These were some of the first such adornments seen in mammals. These head ornaments ranged from pairs of bony ossicones over the nose, eyes, and braincase of *Protoceras* (Late Oligocene, North America) to the long, curved antlers and short, forked nasal horn of *Kyptoceras* (Early Pliocene, Florida).

Synthetoceras was one of the last of this line of ancient, deer-like camels and, at about 6.5 feet (2 m) long, one of the largest of the group. Its head ornamentation also leans to the extreme: a pair of short, curved brow horns and a tremendously long nasal horn that was fused at the base and forked at the top, giving it a Y shape. Horns of this kind were probably a way for the males and females of these animals to identify each other but also may have been used by males in contests over territory or mates. *Synthetoceras* and its relatives had tall, crowned cheek teeth for shearing and grinding tough grasslands vegetation. *Synthetoceras* had four hoofed toes in the front and two in the back, indicating another transition in the direction of the fully two-toed condition seen in camels.

Aepycamelus (Middle to Late Miocene, Colorado). Although modern camels are native today only in arid regions of Asia and Africa, their ancestors originally were a widespread group of successful North American browsers that lived in much less harsh woodlands. Their roots date back to the Late Eocene of North America, in the form of rabbit- and goat-sized animals such as *Protylopus* and *Poebrotherium*. An elongated neck and two hooves on each foot were traits found even in the earliest known camels. Camels continued to evolve into larger forms with longer necks and increasingly specialized adaptations and were restricted to North America until only about 5 million years ago, in the Pliocene Epoch, when they migrated to Asia, Africa, and South America. It is on those three continents that all modern forms (including the South American llama) are now found.

Extant camels no longer have hooves; instead, they have two-toed feet with toenails and foot pads. These traits were present in extinct North American taxa from the Late Miocene such as *Aepycamelus*. *Aepycamelus* was an especially large camel that lived in North America during the Middle and Late Miocene. It was giraffe-like in form, with long, slender legs and a long neck. At about 10 feet (3 m) tall at the head, *Aepycamelus* probably lived a life similar to that of a giraffe.

Fossil **trackways** from Miocene deposits provide evidence that by the time of *Aepycamelus*, camels had developed a specialized form of long-leg running called pacing. To use this gait, which today is used by extant camels and giraffes, the animal alternately moves the legs on one side of the body, fore and hind together, one side at a time. The left legs move together, and then the right legs move together. Moving both the front and hind legs on one side of the body at the same time maximizes the speed that is possible for animals with such long legs. Horses can be trained to use a pacing gait.

The familiar hump of the modern day camel was not present in North American forms. The hump and other anatomical and physiological adaptations that enable the camel to live in harsh, dry environments evolved after these animals migrated to Africa, 5 million years ago. Camels were extinct in North America by the Late Pleistocene.

Megaloceros (Late Pleistocene, Europe). Among the ancestors of true deer were several taxa that developed large bodies and elaborate antlers. *Megaloceros* was one of the most spectacular of these. Antlers differ from the bony bumps and horns of giraffes and cattle in that they are shed annually. Ancestral deer first appeared in Eurasia and later migrated to North America. *Megaloceros* looked very similar to a modern elk but was not a direct elk ancestor. The animal was about 6.5 feet (2 m) tall at the shoulders. Its magnificent antlers could grow to be 12 feet (3.7 m) wide, an astoundingly heavy feature that required the deer to have a robust, muscular neck. Equally surprising is that the large antlers of *Megaloceros* were shed and regrown annually, a fact that has been confirmed by examining many specimens of *Megaloceros*. Some of these specimens show different growth stages of the antlers for animals of the same size. *Megaloceros* is found in many European and Asian locations, ranging from Ireland to Siberia and China. The animal probably lived in herds and was a populous taxon until its gradual decline in the Late Pleistocene—a time when it also was being hunted by early humans. The numbers of *Megaloceros* dropped precipitously about 10,500 years ago, but a recent fossil discovery confirmed that this extinct deer taxon was still alive in the Ural Mountains of Central Asia as recently as 7,000 years ago.

Pelorovis (Middle to Late Pleistocene, Africa). The earliest bovines—we call the living species "cattle" when they are domesticated—were small, cat-sized ruminants from North America such as *Hypertragulus* (Late Eocene to Early Oligocene, North America), but these ancient bovines had largely developed into the ancestors of today's various forms by the Miocene in Europe, Asia, and North Africa. *Pelorovis* was an especially large ancestor of the African buffalo. It had huge, curved, down-turned horns and a body that measured about 10 feet (3 m) long. The total span of the two brow horns may have been up to 12 feet (3.6 m). *Pelorovis* had proportionately longer legs than the modern Cape buffalo. This made *Pelorovis* taller: It stood about 5.3 feet (1.6 m) at the shoulders. Its longer skull and jaws suggest that *Pelorovis* was most at home on the plains, eating short grasses. This is somewhat unlike the modern Cape buffalo, which prefer to eat bunches of longer grasses.

PERISSODACTYLA: RHINOS, HORSES, TAPIRS, AND THEIR ANCESTORS

The odd-toed ungulates known as the perissodactyls—a group with origins in the Late Paleocene of Asia—are not nearly as diverse as they once were. Although the widely dispersed horses continue as one of the most prevalent groups of hoofed mammals, the ancestors of rhinoceroses and tapirs were at one time much more diverse than their descendants are today. Most perissodactyls are three toed, with the middle digit being the most weight bearing. Horses eventually reduced their hooves to a single, broad toe on each foot.

Perissodactyls were the most dominant medium- and large-sized herbivores of the middle to late Cenozoic. Their remains are found in abundance in North America, in Europe, and in Asia, where they originated. Later taxa migrated to and evolved in the continents of the Southern Hemisphere. Most lineages of perissodactyls became extinct. They are survived today only by the horses, the rhinoceroses, and the tapirs. Their current status hardly befits their dominating presence in the early evolution of browsing mammals. Perissodactyls evolved into many diverse and widely distributed forms beginning in the Eocene. These forms included some exceptionally large groups such as the bumpy-headed brontotheres, giant rhinoceroses, and the largest land mammal ever, the rhinoceros-related *Paraceratherium* (previously known as *Indricotherium*) that could eat from treetops that no other animals could reach.

The evolution of horses has a remarkably rich fossil record showing various stages of anatomical changes that led to the modern horse. Emerging from the Early Eocene stock of some of the first perissodactyls, horses began as small browsing animals no bigger than a beagle. From these humble origins developed several lines of horses, not all directly related, that exhibited a set of consistent changes that led to the modern taxa *Equus*. From the Eocene to the emergence of modern horses in the Pleistocene, horses underwent a gradual increase in body size; developed teeth more suited for grazing on grasses than for eating soft, tropical vegetation; and reduced the number of digits (hooves) on their feet from four to the one seen in all modern horses.

Over time, horses developed cheek teeth that were increasingly more **lophodont**: molar teeth with transverse ridges that joined the cusps to create a more effective grinding surface. Horses also benefited from changes to their digestive system that allowed them better to digest the tough, cellulose carbohydrates found in vegetation. These gradual changes, over millions of years, were largely the result of climate changes, as the tropical world of the Eocene gradually gave way to a cooler, less-forested habitat with many grasslands.

Rhinoceroses were a much more diverse group during the Eocene and Miocene Epochs. Known today from only five species that live in Africa and Central Asia, the living rhino is characterized by its familiar nose horn and its thick, armorlike skin. Extinct ancestors of the rhinos include not only this most familiar body form, but also a number of others that seem unlike rhinos in most respects. The evolution of rhinoceroses happened in two distinctive phases. The first phase occurred early, from the Eocene through the Oligocene, in North America and Asia. Taxa from that early radiation included donkey-sized browsers such as *Hyracyus* (Early to Late Eocene, North America, Europe, and Asia) and *Hyracodon* (Early Oligocene to Early Miocene, North America) that had limbs and dentition showing parallels to the evolution of early horses. These same horse-like rhinoceros ancestors also gave rise, during the Oligocene, to a line of giant, browsing, hornless rhinoceroses. Some taxa, such as *Paraceratherium*, were the largest land mammals ever.

In addition to the so-called hyracodonts and indricotheres, another line of early rhinos were the amynodontids: large, stocky, short-legged herbivores that may have had a tapirlike proboscis to aid in grasping leaves and other plants. Amynodonts such as *Meta-mynodon* (Late Eocene to Early Miocene, North America and Asia) had enlarged, tusklike canines reminiscent of the teeth of hippopotamuses. The teeth of amynodonts and the position of their eyes high on the skull suggest that they led a semiaquatic lifestyle not unlike that of hippos—to which, however, they are unrelated.

The first phase of rhinoceros evolution diminished by the end of the Oligocene and overlapped with the second phase that led to modern, horned rhinos. The earliest members of the Rhinocerotidae, the group that includes modern rhinos, date back to the beginning of the Oligocene in North America. Their numbers were limited until a great radiation of many kinds of horned rhinos that took place from the Miocene through to the Pleistocene. Rhinos disappeared from North America by about 5 million years ago, and their numbers greatly declined worldwide. Several North American forms adapted well to the conditions of the Pleistocene Ice Age, however.

Interestingly, the nasal horn of the rhinoceros is not composed of bone, but of thickly matted hair—a feature that normally does not fossilize. Evidence for the presence of such horns is found by examining the bony spots on the skull where the horns were attached. Occasionally, the frozen body of an extinct Pleistocene rhino is found with hair and horn intact. The presence of horned rhinos is also a matter of human prehistory: Such rhinos are recorded in cave paintings across Europe, where these magnificent creatures once lived alongside early humans.

Following are descriptions of representative members of the extinct odd-toed ungulates.

Heptodon (Early Eocene, North America). There is only one genus and four species of living tapirs. Three of these species range from Central to South America; the fourth species lives in Burma (Myanmar) and Thailand. The ancestors of tapirs were one of the earliest groups of perissodactyls. Modern tapirs are donkey-sized, with short, slender legs and a long skull equipped with teeth that resemble those of a horse. Tapirs' feet are hoofed, with four toes on the front feet and three on the hind feet.

A notable novelty of tapir anatomy is a large nasal opening with a small trunk that the animals use to handle the plants that they eat. *Heptodon* was one of the earliest tapirs and—except for the lack of a well-developed nasal trunk—was very similar to modern tapirs. Although only about half the size of a modern tapir, *Heptodon* already had four hoofs on its front feet and three on its back feet. The dental formula of *Heptodon* is close to that of extant tapirs, although modern forms have somewhat more robust cheek teeth than did their earliest ancestors. More modern forms of tapirs, with a proboscis, date from the Early Oligocene. Tapirs were widespread in North America, Europe, and Asia until the Late Pleistocene.

Hyracotherium (Early Eocene, Europe, Asia, and North America). Originally thought to be an ancestor of the hyrax, a small

African mammal, *Hyracotherium* is sometimes known as *Eohippus*, the "dawn horse," because it now is considered to be one of the earliest horse ancestors. As the starting point in horse evolution, *Hyracotherium* provides a suite of primitive features that were modified over time as horses became bigger, faster, and more capable of eating grasses. *Hyracotherium* was the size of a small dog, about 2 feet (60 cm) long. It had a shorter face than later horses and the same number of digits (hooves) on its feet as early tapirs: four on the front and three in the rear. In *Hyracotherium*, however, the digit bearing the most weight was the middle or third one—a trend that gradually led to the reduction of all other toes in horses in favor of a single, enlarged hoof based on the middle toe. The teeth of *Hyracotherium* were low-crowned and conservative; they were suited primarily for eating the soft, tropical vegetation that the animal plucked from the low branches of bushes and trees.

Mesohippus (Middle Oligocene, North America). *Mesohippus* represents an example from the middle period of horse evolution, a time that followed the cooling of habitats and the development of grasslands, two changes that affected the direction of horse anatomy. *Mesohippus* was about twice as large as *Hyracotherium*, with a length of about 4 feet (1.2 m). Its legs were longer and more slender than those of its predecessors, and it was one of the first known horses to have reduced its digits to a more lightweight, three-toed foot. The middle toe was significantly larger than the others. This emphasized its weight-bearing function and led to an increase in the horse's trotting speed.

The jaws of *Mesohippus* were not significantly different from those of *Hyracotherium* and remained best adapted for low browsing. The *Mesohippus* skull was somewhat longer, however, and in *Mesohippus*, the surface area devoted to grinding teeth was increased by a modification of the premolars as part of the chewing battery of cheek teeth. *Mesohippus*'s molars, too, had taken on a more lophodont structure to improve the horse's chewing ability.

By the time of the Miocene and the increasing prevalence of arid grasslands across the Northern Hemisphere, other early horses—including *Parahippus* (Early Miocene, North America) and *Anchitherium* (Early to Late Miocene, North America, Europe, and Asia)—continued the adaptive trends seen in *Mesohippus* and radiated across Europe and Asia.

Hipparion (Middle Miocene to Pleistocene, North America, Europe, Asia, and Africa). *Hipparion* represents one of the last great families of extinct horses just prior to the emergence of *Equus*, the modern horse. Radiating widely across North America, Great Britain, Russia, and China, and even to South Africa, *Hipparion* was about the size of a pony. Known from several different species, *Hipparion* had well-developed lophodont cheek teeth with highly distinctive ridges that made up a formidable grinding surface. These horses had fully adapted to life on the plains. Their feet still retained three digits, but only the enlarged middle hoof was functional and weight bearing. *Hipparion* was among many varieties of grazing horses that were prevalent during the Miocene and Pleistocene. The success of *Hipparion*, along with that of the taxon *Merychippus* (Middle to Late Miocene, North America), led to the rapid radiation of modern horses in the Old World and to South America, as well.

Paraceratherium (Oligocene, Central Asia). *Paraceratherium* was part of the radiation of early hornless ancestors of rhinoceroses. Known from its skull and fragmentary postcranial bones, *Paraceratherium* was a giant among giants. Compared with the largest African elephant on record—an animal that weighed more than 13 tons (14.3 tonnes) and measured 14 feet (4.2 m) tall at the shoulder—*Paraceratherium* was about 40 percent larger: It stood 18 feet (5.4 m) tall at the shoulder and weighed an astonishing 27 tons (30 tonnes). The huge skull of *Paraceratherium* had plant-grinding cheek teeth, a large gap between the premolars, and tusklike incisors that alone made up the dentition at the **anterior** end of the upper and lower jaws. *Paraceratherium* used its front teeth to pluck leaves from treetops that no other animals could reach. The animal's skull also has a large nasal cavity. This cavity probably housed a prehensile, gripping upper lip not unlike that of

Merychippus (Miocene, North America), a horse from the middle period of horse evolution.

the giraffe. The feet had three large hooves each. This presumably gentle, browsing animal was twice as large as the mammoths.

Chalicotherium (Late Oligocene, Asia). The chalicotheres were another group of rather bizarre perissodactyls that have no living relatives. Arising during the Eocene, the chalicotheres were most diverse during the Miocene; a few taxa survived in Africa and Asia until the Pleistocene. The dentition of chalicotheres links them to rhinos and horses. Although odd toed, chalicotheres had bearlike claws instead of hooves like other ungulates. They also were characterized by having forelimbs longer than their hind limbs. The combination of claws and longer forelimbs shows that these animals were not runners. They probably spent their time rooting up plants or pulling down branches from trees to nibble the leaves. They possibly stood on their hind limbs to extend their reach.

Paraceratherium (previously known as *Indricotherium*) (Oligocene, Central Asia) was related to hornless ancestors of rhinoceroses and was the largest terrestrial mammal of all time.

The length of the arms of *Chalicotherium* was extreme, even among chalictotheres. About the size of a large horse, *Chalicotherium* had forelimbs, or arms, that were twice as long as its hind limbs. This gave it a most gorillalike posture. Judging from the robust structure of its hind limbs and pelvic girdle, *Chalicotherium* probably could sit for extended periods as it browsed through trees, possibly rising up to stand or lean against a trunk as its long arms grappled with branches overhead. To this day, in the forests of East Africa, local people still report the presence of a legendary, gorillalike bear called the "Nandi bear" that has some resemblance to *Chalicotherium* except for one "fact": The Nandi bear reportedly is a bloodthirsty carnivore that likes to eat the brains of its victims.

Coelodonta (Late Pleistocene, Europe and Asia). The wooly rhinoceros *Coelodonta* is an Ice Age remnant of the true rhinos. Some frozen specimens have been found with their long, wooly coats and horns intact. One complete specimen was found in the Ukraine, buried in mud, and was so well preserved that its internal organs were in place. At about 12 feet (3.7 m) long and about 5.5 feet (1.6 m) tall at the shoulder, *Coelodonta* had a sturdy torso and short legs. Its long skull was fitted with browsing teeth for eating the tough grasses of the hard, cold grasslands of Eurasia where it remains have been found. *Coelodonta* had two horns. The longer of these was an exceptional 3-foot (0.8 m), curved nasal horn on the tip of the animal's snout. The other horn, about half the length of the first, was positioned between the eyes on the top of the skull. *Coelodonta* was hunted by early humans, and paintings of the animal have been found on cave walls in France.

Elasmotherium (Pleistocene, Europe and Central Asia). *Elasmotherium* was the most monstrous of Pleistocene rhinos. Measuring about 20 feet (6 m) long, it was a native of cold, Ice Age steppe environments where grasses were the main vegetation. Like *Coelodonta*, *Elasmotherium* was coated in thick, wooly fur. The dentition of *Elasmotherium* is unusual in that it totally lacked front teeth—the incisors normally seen in perissodactyls. Lacking incisors, it may have used its lips to pull vegetation out of the ground. Its legs were longer than those of other rhinos and equipped it more for running. At about 5 tons (5.5 tonnes), however, it was not about to run very far. The showpiece of this beast was its enormous single horn. Attached to a broad area on top of the skull, just over the eyes, this wide and robust horn measured about 7 feet (2 m) long—about twice as tall as the skull was long.

Brontops (Early Oligocene, North America). Brontotheres, or "thunder beasts," made up another group of extinct, rhinoceroslike perissodactyls with enormous bodies and unusual skull ornamentation. The brontotheres were most prevalent while their habitats remained moist and semitropical. They fed on the abundance of soft leaves and forest vegetation that their jaws were best equipped to consume. Their reign was short. It lasted little more than 15 million years in North America and Asia. As climates became drier and forests shrank, brontotheres were unable to adapt quickly enough to the changing food supplies. They soon were displaced by better-adapted browsing animals. The brontotheres filled a niche similar to that of the earlier dinoceratans, and they met a similar fate.

About 40 different taxa of brontotheres are known. *Brontops* was one of the later brontotheres. One trend in the evolution of brontotheres was the transformation of the snout region of the skull. Brontotheres from the Early Eocene had long, unadorned, tapirlike snouts. Over time, the snout became shorter, flatter, and broader, and the dentition became more robust, including large, tusklike incisors. A bony bump on top of the snout evolved from a small protuberance in the Late Eocene to an elaborately forked but rounded horn on the nose by the Early Oligocene. In *Brontops*, the two parts of this horn were widely separated and capped by a bulbous, bony knob. The horn probably was covered by skin. It appears that Brontops, like other brontotheres, had a short proboscis or a muscular lip for grappling with food. *Brontops* stood about 8 feet (2.5 m) tall at the shoulder.

Embolotherium (Early Oligocene, Mongolia). The equally large *Embolotherium* had perhaps the most unusual headgear seen in a brontothere. This consisted of a long, bony plate that began as a frill toward the rear of the skull and swept down over the skull cap to form a broad, upright, bony paddle on top of the animal's snout. The name *Embolotherium,* "battering-ram nose beast," was assigned to this brontotheres in 1929 by Henry Fairfield Osborn. Osborn's Asian expeditions of the 1920s had recovered 14 specimens of this unusual brontothere. "This single nasal protuberance," explained Osborn, "is totally different in structure from the paired frontonasal bony horn of all previously known titanotheres." The purpose of this protuberance, he speculated, was to allow *Embolotherium* to batter, assault, attack, and toss opponents during intraspecies contests. While the battering-ram theory indeed makes sense, the horns of brontotheres probably were equally useful for rooting up plants and browsing through bushes and trees as the animal foraged for leaves.

CETACEA: WHALES, DOLPHINS, AND PORPOISES

The relationship of whales, dolphins, and porpoises—fully marine mammals—to the even-toed hoofed mammals is not immediately apparent in a comparison of the morphological features of extant species. That whales are descended from land mammals has long been understood. This understanding is based primarily on the design of whales' skulls, inner-ear bones, and teeth, and on the animals' lack of gill organs for taking in oxygen. Similar cases exist in the annals of early vertebrate history, wherein an adaptive conversion took place from a terrestrial to an aquatic habitat. Which mammals were most closely related to whales long has been a source of debate. A combination of recent fossil evidence and molecular analysis now has confirmed the origins of whales from within the artiodactyls and shown that the whales' closest living terrestrial relatives most likely are the hippopotamuses.

Whales are classified into three groups. The Archaeoceti include ancestral and primitive whales that date primarily from Eocene deposits in Pakistan, Africa, Asia, and North America. The Odontoceti, or toothed whales, extend back to the Oligocene and Miocene of Australia, Asia, North America, and South America. The Mysticeti are the baleen whales; their rise also took place during the Oligocene and Miocene. Modern whales have streamlined bodies and forelimbs modified into paddles. Vestiges of hind limbs are present but not visible on the outside. A whale's skull is fitted with a blowhole for breathing at the water's surface. The only hair on a whale's body is found on the snout.

There currently are 79 living whale species. Most extant whales are toothed. The toothed whales include beaked whales, dolphins, porpoises, and killer whales. The largest whales are baleen, or toothless, whales that feed using a mouth filter. These include gray whales, right whales, humpback whales, and the blue whale. The blue whale is the largest of all living animals, on land or in the sea. It measures about 110 feet (33 m) long and weighs 200 tons (182 tonnes).

A number of fossil taxa from the Eocene effectively illustrate stages in the transition of whale ancestors from a terrestrial to a marine existence. The earliest known whale connection is that of *Himalayacetus* (Early Eocene, India), an animal known only from a few fragments, including part of a lower jaw and a molar. These pieces are enough, however, to connect *Himalayacetus* with the next well-known early whale specimen, that of *Pakicetus*, an animal that lived on land but had a skull with whalelike features. *Ambulocetus* (Middle Eocene, Pakistan), the "limbed whale," was an early whale that had short limbs modified into paddles. It could have walked on land, perhaps in the manner of a sea lion, dragging itself along with its front legs.

In 2003, paleontologist Philip D. Gingerich made a strong case that the Eocene transition of whales from land to sea took place in two phases. The first was a stage during which hind-limb paddling gave way to an undulation of the hips as the primary source of locomotive power, as in *Rodhocetus* (Middle Eocene, Pakistan). The second phase, represented by *Dorudon* (Middle Eocene, North America and Egypt), was a transition to tail-powered swimming as seen in modern whales. *Dorudon* also represented a tendency toward large body size in these early marine mammals; it had a length of about 17 feet (5 m). *Basilosaurus* (Middle Eocene, Egypt) was a still more derived whale. It had hind limbs that were greatly reduced in favor of tail-powered swimming.

The following taxa represent key stages in the evolution of early whales from primitive to modern forms.

Pakicetus (Early Eocene, Pakistan). *Pakicetus* was, essentially, a hoofed mammal that lived on land. Its skull was long and showed early adaptations that would improve its hearing underwater, a clue to the origin of the whales. The shape of the animal's braincase and the teeth, especially the molars, also provide links to the early whales that followed. At about the size of a coyote, *Pakicetus* had short, slender limbs. Its teeth were sharply pointed and primitive, suggesting a predatory lifestyle. While early interpretations of *Pakicetus* pictured it as a semiaquatic animal, new findings have revealed more about its terrestrial nature. The entire skeleton of *Pakicetus* is not known, but recent fieldwork led by paleontologist J.G.M. Thewissen recovered some 150 disarticulated postcranial bones and several partial skulls from a single **bone bed** in Pakistan. Thewissen was able to use the structure of the limbs, knees, and ankles of *Pakicetus* to illustrate that the animal was well adapted for running and possibly jumping, not unlike other early hoofed mammals.

Ambulocetus (Middle Eocene, Pakistan). *Ambulocetus* has been described as a sea-lion-sized mammal with the body of a crocodile but with longer hind limbs for swimming. It had well-developed limbs and large hands and feet that were modified from those of its land-loving forebears. These modified limbs, hands, and feet make this semiaquatic mammal an important transitional fossil that documents a key phase in the evolution of whales from land mammals. Known from a nearly complete specimen, *Ambulocetus* leaves little doubt about the terrestrial origins of whales. This heavy, rotund beast probably was not able to move well on land, although it probably could drag its body about in a manner similar to that of a walrus or a sea lion. Its teeth were sharp and had characteristics that were transitional between those of its terrestrial ancestors—the wolflike Mesonychids—and toothed whales. Its long, muscular jaw was capable of clamping down hard on captured prey. Pictured as a largely aquatic animal, *Ambulocetus* probably lived in a near-shore environment, where it could rest easily on shallow rocks and ledges whenever it grew tired of swimming and paddling. Aquatic adaptations of *Ambulocetus*'s skull included ears for hearing underwater; a nasal passage that allowed the animal to swallow food underwater; and widely spaced, predatory teeth.

Basilosaurus (Late Eocene, Egypt). By the Late Eocene, fully aquatic whales such as *Basilosaurus* had found their niche in the ocean. This large mammal had a long, streamlined body with a relatively small head. Originally thought to be a dinosaur—hence the name, which means "king of the lizards"—*Basilosaurus* turned out to be one of the largest known early whales. Measuring about 80 feet

Basilosaurus (Late Eocene, Egypt) was an early, fully aquatic whale.

(25 m) long, *Basilosaurus* truly was of modern whale proportions. It was a toothed whale with relatively short pectoral paddles. It swam by means of an undulating motion of the pelvic and tail region, in a manner similar to that of modern whales. Remnants of its terrestrial hind limbs, no longer attached to the pelvic region, were greatly reduced but still found inside the body. *Basilosaurus* and other early whales lacked the so-called melon organ that is found in the skulls of modern whales and used for echolocation.

Cetotherium (Middle to Late Miocene, Europe). Modern baleen whales have roots in the Late Oligocene and became widespread in the Miocene and Early Pliocene. Their remains have been found in deposits that represent all of the major oceans of that time span. *Cetotherium* was typical of these early baleen whales. It was a modern but relatively small filter-feeding whale that otherwise had the body plan seen in the extant blue whale. Measuring only about 13 feet (4 m) long, this small whale probably was prey to some of the largest of the sharks with which it shared the ocean.

Eurhinodelphis (Middle to Late Miocene, North America and Asia). Among the early members of the modern toothed whales was *Eurhinodelphis*. This animal was part of a family of dolphin-sized mammals with long, narrow snouts and widely spaced, needlelike teeth. *Eurhinodelphis* was closely related to dolphins and had an ornate ear design that suggests the development of an early version of the echolocation system that is seen in today's dolphins and whales. Its streamlined body and powerful tail fin indicate that *Eurhinodelphis* was a fast-moving predator, skilled at chasing down and snaring fish in its long, toothed beak. The front portion of *Eurhinodelphis*'s snout lacked teeth and may have been used to bat at fish and then direct them into the mouth, where they could be snagged by the animal's teeth.

SUMMARY

This chapter explored the wide range of extinct hoofed mammals and the adaptations that led to their success in many habitats, both terrestrial and aquatic.

1. The Ungulata, or hoofed mammals, is divided into two subgroups. The Cetartiodactyla include the even-toed hoofed mammals such as pigs, camels, deer, giraffes, cattle, goats, antelopes, and many others, plus whales and dolphins (order Cetacea), which are thought to be closely related to hippos. The Perissodactyla include the odd-toed hoofed mammals such as tapirs, rhinoceroses, and horses.
2. The ungulates evolved in the Northern Hemisphere by the Late Paleocene Epoch and eventually migrated south to Africa and South America.
3. Common traits of ungulates can be traced in their robust, plant-eating dentition; their multichambered digestive tracts; and an assortment of horns, antlers, and other head ornaments.

4. Today, artiodactyl taxa outnumber perissodactyl taxa by about thirteen to one.

5. Most perissodactyls are three toed, with the middle digit being the most weight bearing. Horses eventually reduced their hooves to a single, broad toe on each foot.

6. Over time, hoofed mammals developed cheek teeth that were increasingly more lophodont: molar teeth with transverse ridges joining the cusps, thereby creating a more effective grinding surface.

7. Evidence that whales are descended from land mammals is largely understood and primarily based on the design of their skulls, their inner-ear bones, their teeth, and their lack of gill organs for breathing in water. Phylogenetic trees produced by molecular analyses offer new hypotheses that need to be tested by morphological evidence issued from the fossil record.

8. A combination of recent fossil evidence and molecular analysis has confirmed the origins of whales from within the artiodactyls and has shown that their closest living relatives are most likely the hippopotamuses.

6

MAMMOTHS, ELEPHANTS, AND THEIR RELATIVES: THE PAENUNGULATA

Elephants and their relatives make up the group of mammals known as the **Paenungulata.** The name conferred on this group of seemingly diverse lineage means "almost ungulates"; the animals in the group are connected by certain traits of their jaws and wrists. Among the paenungulates are such familiar extinct members of modern families as the mastodonts and wooly mammoths. The group also includes some spectacular surprises in the form of extinct marine mammals and large, horned, elephantlike browsers.

The Paenungulata are divided into five groups. The Proboscidea ("trunk feeders") include the elephants. The Sirenia include manatees, dugongs, and other animals popularly known as "sea cows." The Hyracoidea are the small, rabbit-sized hyraxes. Two extinct groups are the Embrithopoda—a group of horned, elephantlike browsers—and the Desmostylia, an extinct group of marine mammals.

THE PROBOSCIDEA: ELEPHANTS OLD AND NEW

The proboscideans, or elephants, may have originated in northern Africa, where most of their early evolutionary history is currently known. Fossil remains of elephants are abundant; this is due largely to the hefty nature of their bones and teeth, which are more likely than the remains of smaller animals to be preserved. More than 170 species of fossil proboscids have been described, many from teeth alone, but a large number also are known from well-preserved diagnostic elements beyond elephant dentition. The remains of mammoths that once roamed the cold northern reaches of the Ice Age world are sometimes found frozen with hair and organs intact. Despite the great diversity of elephants in the past, only one extant taxon remains. It includes three living species found in Africa and Asia.

Traits shared by proboscideans include an enlargement of the skull; the presence of a trunk; a short neck; and long, pillarlike legs with feet flattened to support a large body. In proboscid jaws, the second pair of upper incisors became elongated to form tusks. Overall, the dental formula was reduced to mostly large, grinding molars. As proboscids evolved, proboscid molars became deeper, wider, and more ridged and developed clearly lophodont grinding surfaces.

The ancestral proboscids are known primarily from teeth found in the Late Paleocene and Eocene of Morocco. These early proboscids included pig-sized animals that may have lived in freshwater lakes and ponds. *Moeritherium,* from the Late Eocene of Africa, is better known in the fossil record; it had a body like that of a small hippo and stood barely 2 feet (60 cm) tall at the shoulder.

By the Early Oligocene, the early proboscids were emerging from northern African and splitting into two basic groups, the Deinotheriidae and the Elephantiformes. Deinotheres were Old World proboscids; they are known from their distinguishing lower tusks that curled beneath the chin and from their lack of upper tusks. Deinotheres were extinct by the Middle Pleistocene. By the Middle Miocene, land connection established between Africa and Eurasia and North America allowed proboscideans to migrate across Europe, Asia, and North America.

The elephantiforms radiated rapidly out of the Old World beginning in the Early Miocene. This group included four unique lineages that arose from a common ancestor. The Mammutidae, or mastodonts, were known for their low-crowned and rounded cheek teeth and their sometimes enormously elongated tusks. The Gomphotheriidae were the most common and dominant of the

Moeritherium (Late Eocene to Early Oligocene, Africa)

large mammals found in Europe and Asia during the Miocene. Gomphotheres are noted for having broad trunks and shorter upper tusks than other elephantiforms. They also are known for either an elongated extension of the lower jaw with straight or shovel-like tusks or a shorter lower jaw that gave them a superficial resemblance to modern elephants.

The Stegodontidae were most similar to modern elephants. The Stegodontidae had smaller bodies, a short lower jaw, and short, upwardly turned tusks. Their molars were finely ridged for grinding grasses; this was an advance over earlier, more primitive elephants. The Elephantidae were the fourth group of elephantiforms. This group included the mammoths, with their high-domed skulls, enormous cheek teeth, and long, inwardly curving tusks. Modern elephants had their origins with the elephantids.

Elephant taxa in the Northern Hemisphere—an assortment that included mastodonts, mammoths, and gomphotheres—became extinct with the advancing Pleistocene Ice Age. Some forms of gomphotheres migrated successfully to South America when a land connection between North and South America permitted their entry from the north about 3.5 million years ago. These elephants were extinct by the beginning of the Pleistocene, however. The only line of elephants to survive was the remnant of the elephantiforms that remained in the warmer climates of Africa. Although related to the mammoths of the north, these modern elephants adapted to the warmer climates, and their descendants still live in the Old World.

Daouitherium (Early Eocence, Morocco). Along with *Phosphatherium,* which is found in the same and slightly older fossil deposits of North Africa, *Daouitherium* is one of the earliest known true proboscideans. *Daouitherium* also is one of the oldest known large mammals of Africa and is much larger than *Phosphatherium.* Although a definition of "large" in this case is somewhat relative, *Daouitherium* had a lower jaw that measured 8 inches (20 cm) long. The animal was about the size of a pig and may have weighed about 66 pounds (30 kg). This made it twice the size of *Phosphatherium.* Known from lower jaws with intact dentition, the recently discovered *Daouitherium* shows that the radiation of proboscideans of various sizes occurred earlier in the Cenozoic than previously had been thought and strongly supports a Paleocene origin of early elephants coming out of Africa. The teeth of *Daouitherium* are not as broad as in later proboscideans but are mildly ridged, thus showing an early stage in the evolution of the robust, lophodont teeth of later elephants.

Moeritherium (Late Eocene to Early Oligocene, Africa). *Moeritherium* is one of the better-known primitive elephants. It represents a stage during which these animals were beginning to attain both larger body size and the dental adaptations seen later in true elephants. *Moeritherium's* head was greatly elongated and resembled that of a tapir. Although not necessarily a direct ancestor of proboscideans, *Moeritherium* exhibited many traits that would appear in true proboscideans in more exaggerated form. *Moeritherium* possessed six small molar teeth on both sides of its upper and lower jaws. In proboscideans, this dental formula developed into a single, exceptionally large molar. The animal's upper incisors were enlarged but not yet especially tusklike. The postcranial skeleton of *Moeritherium* was more hippolike than elephantlike, with short limbs, a longer neck, and only a faint hint of the long, treelike legs and extremely short and heavily muscled neck found in related elephants.

Deinotherium (Miocene to Pleistocene, Europe and Asia). *Deinotherium* ("terrible beast") was from an Old World group of early proboscids that was not directly related to the elephantiforms. These large proboscideans lived during the height of the early radiation of elephants and their kin. Found in such widespread localities as Germany, India, and Kenya, *Deinotherium* had a pair of sharply downturned lower tusks that curved back under its chin. It is one of the largest known proboscids, with a shoulder height of 11.5 feet (3.5 m)—about 33.3 feet (1 m) taller than the average living African elephant. The function of the tusks of *Deinotherium* is a matter of spirited speculation. They could have been used to root up plants from the ground, to drag down low-hanging tree branches, or perhaps even to strip trees of soft, edible bark.

Gomphotherium (Early Miocene to Early Pliocene, Europe, Africa, North America, and Asia). *Gomphotherium* was a single taxon within the gomphotheres, one of the four subgroups in the group elephantiforms. *Gomphotherium* was moderately large; it measured about 6.6 feet (2 m) at the shoulder. Its most distinctive features were two pairs of tusks that adorned its upper and lower jaws. The upper tusks were somewhat straight or downturned, but the two closely paired lower tusks were extensions of an extremely long lower jawbone. *Gomphotherium* probably rooted up plants and roots with its lower, shovel tusks and then drew this food into its mouth with its long trunk and steadying upper tusks. One later gomphothere taxon, called *Platybelodon* (Late Miocene, Europe, Mongolia, and Africa), had an even broader and more shovel-like pair of lower tusks that were widely flattened, making them excellent scoops.

Amebelodon (Late Miocene, North America). *Amebelodon* ("shovel tusk") was a later North American taxon of gomphothere. About as large as the modern African elephant, it had some of the longest and most broadly flattened shovel tusks of the gomphotheres. It presumably used these tusks to scrape up soft, aquatic plants as it waded in lakes and streams. The lower tusks of *Amebelodon* were about as long, but not as wide as, those of *Platybelodon*. The ends of *Amebelodon*'s lower tusks were chiseled with wear; this wear formed a fine, beveled edge that was well suited for uprooting and severing rooted plants, branches, and other vegetation. The upper tusks of *Amebelodon*, like those of *Platybelodon*, were short compared with those of earlier gomphotheres.

Mammut (Late Miocene to Late Pleistocene, North America). *Mammut* was a true mastodont ("nipple tooth"), a wide ranging member of the Mammutidae that roamed North America into and during the Late Pleistocene Ice Age. Not to be confused with the wooly mammoth—its elephantiform cousin, with which it shared its habitat—the mastodont was characterized by the blunt, conical shape of its cheek teeth and long tusks that were straighter than those of the mammoth. *Anancus* (Pliocene-Pleistocene, Europe) was a European cousin of *Mammut* whose long tusks reached 10 feet (3 m) and so were about as long as *Anancus* was tall. *Mammut* measured about 10 feet (3 m) tall at the shoulder and had a wooly coat. Its teeth were best suited for chewing spruce leaves and other soft vegetation, in contrast with the more extremely ridged teeth of the mammoth, which were better adapted for grazing on tough grasses and ground cover. Some hairless taxa of mastodonts are known from Africa, Asia, and Europe.

Mammuthus (Middle Pleistocene, Europe, Asia, and North America). *Mammuthus*, the wooly mammoth and its direct ancestors, are extinct members of the elephantiforms. Living in some habitats alongside their mastodont cousins, mammoths and all elephantiforms were characterized by a further elaboration of elephantiform cheek teeth. The molars were tall and broad, with deep ridges covered with tough enamel. These characteristics made them suitable for grinding tough, dry vegetation such as the grasses, tree bark, and branches found in the cold, steppe woodlands of the Northern Hemisphere.

Several species of mammoth lived throughout North America, Europe, and Asia until about 3,500 years ago, following the last Ice Age. The earliest mammoths were not coated in fur; that development took hold as the Ice Age set in, about 700,000 years ago. The familiar wooly mammoth had long, inwardly or upwardly curving tusks that were up to 16 feet (5 m) long. Mammoths became extinct after the last Ice Age. The extinction process may have combined the warming of the animals' habitat with overhunting by humans and possible widespread disease. Most mammoths were not as large as modern elephants, although one species from North America reached a shoulder height of 13 feet (4 m).

THE SIRENIA: SEA COWS

Manatees and dugongs are the only surviving taxa of the Sirenia, or sea cows. These animals are large, rotund, fully aquatic mammals with forelimbs modified into flippers and a wide, flat, horizontal tail. They move about slowly, propelling themselves through warm, coastal waters with their tails and steering with their flippers. In contrast to their fatty appearance, these animals actually have quite muscular torsos that enable them to glide effortlessly through the shallow coastal waters and freshwater inlets that they inhabit. These herbivores have reduced dentition that is suited for eating soft aquatic plants and skulls that are modified with high nostrils to allow the animals to breathe air at the surface without having to fully expose the head. Evidence that these animals' terrestrial ancestors once had hind limbs is found in the form of small leg-bone fragments embedded in the muscle of the torso. These fragments once would have been associated with the pelvis.

Sirenians are first known from the Early Eocene, a time when their earliest known members still had four short legs. Modern forms were in place as early as the Late Eocene, after which sirenians radiated widely for a time during the Miocene. Some recent examples, such as the gigantic Stellar's sea cow (Pliocene to recent, Arctic), became extinct as late as 1768. Stellar's sea cow rivaled its largest known extinct ancestors in size; it measured 26 feet (7.9 m) long and weighed an astounding 3 tons (3.3 tonnes).

Pezosiren (Early Eocene, Jamaica). The Caribbean island of Jamaica is not well known for its fossil finds, but in 2001 it was the location of a spectacular discovery that dated back to the earliest days of the sirenians. It was in Jamaica that paleontologist Daryl Domning discovered the nearly complete skeleton of *Pezosiren*, a four-legged ancestor of modern sea cows that in body form—four short legs and a rotund body—resembled a small hippo. Measuring about 7 feet (2.1 m) long and weighing a few hundred pounds, *Pezosiren* represents a remarkable stage in the transition of this family of terrestrial mammals to a fully aquatic life. One aquatic adaptation already in place was a pair of enlarged nostrils that extended back into the skull to make it easier for the animal to take large breaths. *Pezosiren*'s bulbous body most likely provided enough weight to allow the animal to walk confidently in deep water and also provided enough buoyancy to keep the creature afloat and swimming if the need arose.

HYRACOIDEA: THE HYRAXES

All modern forms of hyraxes live in Africa and the Middle East. They are small, rotund, short-limbed, rabbit-sized herbivorous mammals with thick fur and short tails. A modern hyrax somewhat resembles a bobcat with a guinea pig head. Extinct forms were much more diverse. The Hyracoidea had origins in the Late Eocene, with various forms radiating from Africa into Europe and Asia during the Oligocene and Miocene. Some extinct hyraxes were tapir- and horse-sized. They were important grazers and browsers until, eventually, they were displaced by ungulates in most of the niches they occupied. What remained were only six species of small, tree-climbing animals.

Anatomical links between the hyraxes and the elephants include small tusks, toenails instead of hooves, and padded feet. The hyraxes are most closely allied with the sirenians, with which they share a common ancestor.

Kvabebihyrax (Late Pliocene, Europe). *Kvabebihyrax* was about 5 feet, 4 inches (1.6 m) long and resembled a small, furry hippopotamus. It had large, tusklike upper incisors and eyes placed high on the skull behind a moderately long snout. Its lower incisors were broad and protruding. *Kvabebihyrax* was an herbivorous rooter and browser.

Antilohyrax (Late Eocene, Egypt). Extinct hyracoids found in the plentiful Fayum deposits of Egypt ranged widely in size, from an estimated 14 pounds (6.5 kg) for the dog-sized *Thyrohyrax* to an enormous 2,200 pounds (1,000 kg) for *Titanohyrax*. Most, however, averaged a few hundred pounds. The recently described *Antilohyrax* ranks as a smaller member of the group. With a skull about 10 inches (23 cm) long, the whole animal was about the size of a medium-sized dog. *Antilohyrax* is known from a well-preserved skull that is long and narrow. Among the unique traits of *Antilohyrax* were two pairs of upper incisors, the center two of which were the longer, tusklike teeth seen in other hyraxes. The tusks made contact with a sickle-shaped dental pad at the front of the lower jaw. The cheek teeth were low crowned. Combined with the cropping incisors, these cheek teeth probably made *Antilohyrax* adept at eating leaves and other foliage.

EMBRITHOPODA: EXTINCT RHINOLIKE BROWSERS

This extinct group of paenungulates is known mostly from one spectacular taxon from the Early Oligocene of Egypt: the huge, horned, herbivorous *Arsinoitherium*. Fragmentary evidence of more primitive and hornless embrithopods, including *Hypsamasia* (Middle Eocene, Turkey), has been found in Romania and Turkey. Embrithopods have no known living descendants. They are considered a primitive group at the base of the paenungulates, perhaps most closely related to the proboscideans. Embrithopods have neither tusks nor enlarged canines; their cheek teeth are uniformly shaped and high crowned. In their jaws there was no gap between the anterior teeth that were used for cropping and the premolars that were used for grinding vegetation.

Arsinotherium (Early Oligocene, Egypt). *Arsinotherium* was one of the more bizarre-looking proboscideans. Its trunk consisted of little more than a tapirlike flap that covered the front teeth. Its body was rhinolike, but the comparison ends there. On the top of its head, between the eyes and the nostrils, stood was a pair of massive, bony horns. Unlike the horns of true rhinoceroses, which are made up of matted hair, these were composed of bone. Evidence of blood vessels at the base of the horns indicates that they probably were skin covered in life. These horns also were hollow, which reduced their weight somewhat. The horns were joined at the base. On top of the skull, between the two large horns and the eyes, were two smaller bony knobs.

The cheek teeth of *Arsinotherium* were high-crowned and robust, much more so than the teeth of some of its browsing contemporaries. This dentition gave it an advantage in eating tough vegetation. The shoulder height of *Arsinotherium* was about 6 feet (1.8 m). Its skull was tall and heavy and was suspended from a short neck. Because its hind limbs were longer than its forelimbs, *Arsinotherium* had a posture that leaned forward and toward the ground. The animal's horns were more than 2 feet (61 cm) tall on a skull that was only about 30 inches (75 cm) long. The entire animal was about 11 feet (3.4 m) long.

DESMOSTYLIA: HIPPOLIKE WADING BROWSERS

Desmostylians were another group of hippolike, semiaquatic mammals. Like the embrithopods, the desmostylians have no living relatives. Only about six taxa are known, and they have been found only in fossil deposits of the North Pacific Ocean that date from the Oligocene and Miocene. Desmostylians had well-developed forelimbs and hind limbs, with paddlelike hands and feet for swimming. Because the feet were in-turned and the ankles fused, desmostylians could turn only by rotating the whole leg. The animals' dentition included somewhat elongated and robust upper and lower incisors and canines, with the lower set protruding. The molars were unique among mammals: They consisted of joined vertical columns of dentine that formed a low-crowned grinding surface suited for the consumption of soft, aquatic plants and sea grasses. The long anterior teeth could have been used to gather and crop vegetation.

Paleoparadoxia (Miocene, Japan). *Paleoparadoxia* is known from a fairly complete skull and postcranial skeleton. It was a stout animal, with short limbs adapted for swimming. Unlike the sirenians—in which locomotion is powered by a strong, horizontally positioned tail—the desmostylians used their strong forelimbs to provide thrust and their hind limbs for steering. *Paleoparadoxia* was moderately sized, with a skull about 16 inches (40 cm) long. It probably could waddle onto land to rest or sun itself like a walrus but would return to the water to feed on soft plants that it snatched with its long anterior teeth from just below the surface.

Desmostylus (Miocene, Japan and Pacific North America). *Desmostylus* is another well-known member of this clan. Larger than *Paleoparadoxia*, *Desmostylus* measured about 6 feet (1.8 m) long. It had the characteristic in-turned feet of desmosylians coupled with a long neck and a skull with protruding incisors and molars made up of a unique fusion of tubelike dentine structures. The diet and lifestyle of *Desmostylus* and its kin have been a source of speculation for many years. Because the specimens have been found in what once were near-shore habitats, scientists have assumed that the animals were partly aquatic and partly terrestrial. In 2003, to shed some light on the animal's lifestyle, a team of paleontologists led by Mark Clementz of the University of Wyoming analyzed the carbon, oxygen, and strontium isotope compositions of the tooth enamel of *Desmostylus* and other marine and terrestrial mammals of its time. The isotope composition of tooth enamel is greatly affected by the food that an animal eats. In this case, the composition of

Desmostylus's enamel can be compared to the chemical composition of a variety of animals that ate land and water plants. The isotope evidence strongly suggested that *Desmostylus* spent most of its time foraging for plants in freshwater or estuarine (the area in which the freshwater of a river meets the saltwater of the sea) ecosystems.

SUMMARY

This chapter looked at elephants and their relatives, the group of mammals known as the Paenungulata ("almost ungulates").

1. The Paenungulata are divided into five groups. Three groups—the Proboscidea (elephants); the Sirenia (sea cows); and the Hyracoidea (hyraxes)—have living relatives. Two groups are extinct: the Embrithopoda (horned, elephantlike browsers) and the Desmostylia (marine mammals).

2. The elephantiforms radiated rapidly out of the Old World, beginning in the Early Miocene.

3. Elephantiforms include four unique lineages that arose from a common ancestor: the mastodonts, the gomphotheres, the stegodonts, and the elephantids (mammoths and living elephants).

4. Manatees and dugongs are the only surviving taxa of the Sirenia, or sea cows. Sirenians are first known from the Early Eocene, when their earliest known members still had four short legs.

5. All modern forms of hyraxes are small, rotund, short-limbed, rabbit-sized herbivorous mammals that live in Africa and the Middle East. Extinct forms were more diverse; they lived from the Late Eocene to the Miocene and ranged in size from rabbit-sized animals to some as large as small horses.

6. Embrithopods have no known living descendants and are considered a primitive group at the base of the paenungulates. They are perhaps most closely related to the proboscideans. The embrithopods included large, rhinolike browsers with enormous, hollow, bony horns.

7. Desmostylians were a group of hippolike, semiaquatic mammals and have no living relatives. Found only in fossil deposits of the North Pacific Ocean that date from the Oligocene and Miocene, desmostylians had well-developed forelimbs and hind limbs; paddlelike hands and feet for swimming; and unique cheek teeth made up of fused, tubular structures composed of dentine.

7

Big Cats, Hyenas, Dogs, Bears, and Their Relatives: The Carnivores and Creodonts

Large-bodied meat eaters evolved on several occasions in the early Cenozoic history of mammals. Predators with pouches—carnivorous marsupials—evolved independently in both South America (as described in Chapter 1) and Australia (as described in Chapter 2). These marsupial predators sometimes reached the size of lions and exhibited convergent trends with northerly placental predators, such as the development of long, saber-tooth canine teeth. The early hoofed mammals known as condylarths (see Chapter 3) included several large-bodied predators such as the monstrous *Andrewsarchus*. The evolution of the cetacea—whales and dolphins (see Chapter 5)—also includes several distinctly carnivorous taxa.

Two additional groups of specialized predatory mammals with roots in the Paleocene are the **Creodonta** and the **Carnivora**. These two groups arose from a common ancestor but are otherwise unrelated, and only the true carnivores have living members still: dogs, cats, hyenas, and bears. This chapter explores the evolution and lifestyles of these important groups of predatory mammals.

CREODONTA: ONCE-DOMINANT PREDATORS

The extinct Creodonta lived from the Paleocene to the late Miocene and were the dominant carnivorous mammals of North America, Africa, Europe, and Asia during the early Cenozoic. Creodonts often achieved exceptional size, as in the African taxon *Megistoth-erium*, a creature that, at about 18 feet (5.4 m) long, was the equivalent of a bison-sized tiger. The creodonts eventually were replaced in their ecological niche by the Carnivora, whose larger brains, more adaptable dentition, and flexible foot structure gave them several advantages over creodonts.

Creodonts once were thought to be the direct ancestors of the Carnivora, but it has been determined that creodonts and carnivores were not directly related. They probably were descended from a common ancestor, however. In each case, creodonts and carnivores, there arose a great similarity of body types, including dog, bear, and hyena forms.

Creodonts had relatively small brains for their body size. This implies that their senses may not have been as keen as those of carnivores. The creodont jaw had cutting cheek teeth set far back in the jaw. This dentition made it difficult for them to consume anything but meat. In contrast, true carnivores have more varied dentition; this makes them omnivorous and gives them more dietary options. As for locomotion, most creodonts had plantigrade feet—they walked flat-footed, with the soles of their feet on the ground. (The creodont subgroup known as the hyaenodonts was an exception.) Carnivores such as tigers and wolves are digitigrade: They walk on their toes. This makes them faster, quieter, and more agile than animals that must plant the flat of the foot on the ground with every step.

Creodonts were well adapted for carnivory. Known from more than 50 taxa, they generally had short legs; they also had short faces with powerful jaws and teeth for crunching bones and shearing flesh. Two subgroups of creodonts are known. The Oxyaenidae lived during the Paleocene and Eocene of North America and Central Asia and included catlike and bearlike forms. Some taxa were quite large, such as *Sarkastodon* (Late Eocene, Mongolia), an uncannily bearlike beast that measured about 10 feet (3 m) long.

A second subgroup of creodonts was the Hyaenodontidae, which survived until the Late Miocene in the Old World. Three lines of hyaenodontids are recognized. One line featured the brief appearance of saber-toothed forms in the Late Eocene of North America. A second type of hyaenodontid included dog- and civet-sized forms. The third and best-known form was the hyaenodonts. These were large predators that roamed across North America, Eurasia, and Africa and that have been likened in form and lifestyle to today's wolves and hyenas.

Oxyaena (Early Eocene, North America). *Oxyaena* was part of the Oxyaenidae subgroup of creodonts. This wolverine-sized animal had a short face, well-developed canine teeth, cheek teeth with cutting edges for shearing meat, and powerful jaws. Short-limbed and flat-footed, it would have scampered about its woodland habitat preying on other small mammals.

Hyaenodon (Late Eocene to Early Miocene, North America, Europe, Asia, and Africa). *Hyaenodon* ("hyena tooth") was one of the creodont forms known as hyaenodontids. Larger and more agile than the oxyaenids, these predators somewhat resembled a cross between a dog and hyena, only supersized. The largest known specimen of *Hyaenodon* was about 10 feet (2 m) long, the size of a horse. *Hyaenodon* had longer limbs than most creodonts and walked on its toes in digitigrade fashion. This improved its ability to run, although the wide spread of its toes hindered it from being a fast runner. The toes of *Hyaenodon* had blunt claws that were unlike those seen in true Carnivora and would not have been particularly useful in capturing prey. The long, narrow jaws and snout on *Hyaenodon*'s oversized head, coupled with its often-overpowering size, appear to have been this animal's chief offensive weapons.

Megistotherium (Miocene, Egypt). *Megistotherium* was another enormous hyaenodont and possibly the largest predatory mammal ever. (This is a competition being held solely in the imaginations of paleontologists, who like to compare *Megistotherium* to the equally monstrous and much earlier *Andrewsarchus* of Mongolia.) At possibly up to 18 feet (5.5 m) long and with a weight of 1,900 pounds (880 kg), *Megistotherium* is thought to have been larger than a rhinoceros. The *Megistotherium* skull alone was about 3.3 feet (1 m) long. Such body measurements are speculative because little has been found of *Megistotherium* other than its skull, jaws, and teeth. Like other hyaenodonts, *Megistotherium* had a large head with a long, narrow jaw lined with meat-shearing molars and large canines. This

THINK ABOUT IT

Mammal Killers

Before the creodonts and saber-toothed cats became the dominant predators of the mammal world, a host of carryovers from the Mesozoic successfully filled the void left vacant by the extinction of the theropod dinosaurs. Mammals were not the only survivors of the K-T extinction that killed the dinosaurs. Even as mammals strove, during the early Cenozoic, to emerge the shadow of the dinosaurs, they shared their brave new world with equally successful reptile and bird survivors.

Birds also benefited from the void created by the extinction of carnivorous dinosaurs. Having evolved from small theropods themselves, birds were well in advance of mammals when it came to developing a largely predatory lifestyle. By the Early Eocene, the giant, flightless bird *Gastornis* (Late Paleocene to Middle Eocene, Europe) and its cousin *Diatryma* (Middle Eocene, North America) had developed into the most dominant predatory animals in their habitats. Standing up to 7 feet (2 m) tall, these birds had long, muscular legs to carry them as they chased mammals across woodlands and plains, ultimately using their talons and beaks to hold and dismember their catch. These birds also may have hunted in ambush, waiting for herds of small, grazing mammals to pass by before lunging out with their beaks to snap up victims. Such may have been the fate of early horses and other small herbivores that lived among these birds. *Gastornis* and its kind eventually were displaced by creodonts and other mammalian predators. As mammals became larger and more formidable opponents, they turned the tables on the big birds and finally drove them into extinction.

Crocodiles have ancient roots. They persist to this day in limited numbers and in mostly watery, tropical habitats. During the Eocene, however,

was a dental battery suitable for either killing or scavenging. *Megistotherium* was presumably digitigrade, with slender limbs, and so capable of running. Its large size probably precluded it from chasing

Pristichampus (Eocene, North America, Eurasia), a large crocodile that preyed on mammals

several large crocodile species in North America and Europe that had become well adapted to living on dry land made terrors of themselves in a world of small, grazing mammals. *Pristichampus* (Eocene, North America, Eurasia) was one such reptile. Measuring about 10 feet (3 m) long, *Pristichampus* was a running crocodile more at home on land than in the water. Its feet had hooflike nails instead of claws to improve its traction. Because *Pristichampus* had longer legs than an aquatic crocodile, it could easily raise its belly off the ground for long pursuits. Among *Pristichampus*'s chosen prey was probably the early horse *Hyracotherium*, a mini-equine that stood only about 20 inches (8 cm) tall at the shoulder. This small horse would have been a mere morsel for the enormous *Pristichampus*.

prey for too long of a time, however. A lifestyle as an opportunistic hunter and scavenger, similar to that of some modern cats and hyenas, makes sense when interpreting the hyaenodonts.

CARNIVORA: TRUE CATS, DOGS, HYENAS, BEARS, AND SEALS

Except for carnivorous marsupials, most extant meat-eating mammals are members of the Carnivora ("meat eaters"). The ancestors of modern carnivores date back to the Early Paleocene. These ancestors consisted of small, primitive forms that broke, very early on, into the roots of the two main groups of carnivores: the Feliformes (cats, civets, and hyenas) and the Caniformes (dogs, weasels, and bears). The extant groups Felidae and Canidae are the living representatives of these clans. The story does not end with cats and dogs, however, because Carnivora also includes other familiar meat-eating mammals such as bears, weasels, otters, seals, sea lions, and walrus. A few members, such as pandas and badgers, do not even eat meat.

The traits that unite the carnivores are primarily in their dentition. All carnivores, living and extinct, have a pair of carnassial, or meat-shearing, teeth on each side of the jaw. Each pair consists of an enlarged upper premolar and a correspondingly large lower molar; when the jaw is closed to bring them together, these teeth act like two pairs of flesh-cutting scissors. Carnassial teeth are found in all members of the Carnivora except certain taxa, such as seals, in which the meat-shearing teeth were lost secondarily as part of an adaptation for another kind of diet, such as the seals' diet of fish.

Other shared dental traits of true carnivores include sharp incisors for nipping and holding prey and large canine teeth for attacking. Canines, but not felines, also developed large, crushing molars at the back of the jaw that were good for smashing or gnawing on bones. Another difference between feliforms and caniforms involves the bony structure of the inner ear. The inner ear was enclosed in cartilage in felids, but in canids, it was enclosed in bone.

In addition to the terrestrial feliforms and caniforms, a third clade of true carnivores includes the aquatic Pinnipedia, a group composed of seals, sea lions, and walrus. These marine taxa evolved from the bear branch of the caniforms and entered the water by the Late Oligocene; their earliest members have been found in California.

Carnivores arose from insectivore ancestors that had become well established by the Early Paleocene. The basal carnivores of the Paleocene were small and catlike and lived in the shadows of the more dominant creodont predators. The roots of the feliforms and caniforms are both found in the fossil fauna of North America and Eurasia. The rise of the true carnivores began during the Oligocene, as they gradually displaced the diminishing creodonts and radiated widely in the continents of the Old and New Worlds.

Saber-Tooth Adaptations

A familiar feature of several carnivore taxa is the greatly enlarged upper canines found in the so-called saber-toothed cats. Saber-tooth dentition is not unique to one particular animal; it has evolved several times in mammals, each time independently. In addition to the saber-toothed cats of North America and Europe, a similar adaptation arose in the marsupials of South America, including *Thylacosmilus,* from the Late Miocene of Argentina. Even among the true carnivores, saber teeth arose at least twice, once in the earliest feliforms, known as Nimravidae, and again in the family of true cats, the Felidae.

The way in which the saber-tooth dentition was used has been a source of debate for many years. Modern cats such as leopards and lions use a variety of techniques to kill their prey. Unlike hyenas, which routinely grapple with prey animals and begin to eat them before they have died, modern cats usually kill prey animals first and then eat them. In cats, this generally translates into killing methods that are swift and efficient. The anatomy of big cats reveals how the killing is done. The cats first use their muscular forelimbs and large claws to secure the prey and follow up with a killing blow or bite. There is no universal killing blow that is used by all big cats. A clinching bite to the throat, resulting in the rapid suffocation of the prey, is common; this bite often follows a struggle as the cat secures it victim. Lions also are known to suffocate antelope by wrestling them to the ground and clamping the prey's nose and mouth shut with their jaws. An even more specialized killing technique is used by the South American jaguar: After dragging down a prey animal such as a capybara, the cat delivers a bite to the skull that pierces the brain through the ears and quickly kills the animal.

The traditional view of saber-toothed cats was that they were grapple-and-bite predators not unlike extant big cats. This is plausible in some cases, as when the saber-toothed cat might have attacked a moderately sized mammal such as a small horse by dragging it down with its claws and then delivering a suffocating bite to the throat. Larger prey, such as small elephants and rhinoceroses, were another matter, however. Trying to drag such animals down with a bite certainly would have resulted in many broken saber teeth, but this generally is not what is found in the fossil record.

If a prey animal was too large to be dragged down, the cat could have used its saber teeth to rip a wound in the animal instead, so that the prey eventually would bleed to death. The jaws of the saber-toothed cat were particularly well adapted for this tactic. With a wide gape and a muscular bite, a saber-toothed cat could lash out at prey with its jaws, effectively slicing off a chunk of meat even as the victim made its futile escape, fated eventually to succumb to its wounds.

Following are representative examples of fossil taxa from the record of Carnivora.

Hesperocyon (Middle Eocene, North America). One of the earliest members of the caniforms was *Hesperocyon*, a small mammal with a long body and short legs, not unlike a mongoose or a civet. It had a long neck and tail and was about the size of a fox. Unlike feliforms (cats), caniforms (dogs) developed large, crushing molars in the rear of the jaw. An early sign of such development can be seen in the jaws of *Hesperocyon*.

Proailurus (Late Oligocene to Early Miocene, Europe). *Proailurus* is the earliest known true cat and is well represented by fossils from France. It was about the size of an ocelot and had short, strong limbs. Its feet were not yet entirely digitigrade like those of all modern cats. This was a possibly advantage because it provided *Proailurus* with a broader, stronger foot for climbing trees, and *Proailurus* may have specialized in chasing small, arboreal mammals into the trees. *Proailurus* looked much like a modern cat and was about 35 inches (90 cm) long. Its skull showed early modification of the inner-ear cavity that was further developed in later cats. Its jaw had not yet reduced its number of teeth to that seen in later feliforms.

Barbourofelis (Late Miocene, North America). *Barbourofelis*, a long-legged animal about the size of a lion, was a nimravid. The nimravids were a group of early feliforms that convergently developed long, saber-tooth dentition similar to that of the unrelated true cats. *Barbourofelis* was one of the last members of this group, which first appeared in the Late Eocene and eventually was displaced by the more abundant true cats. *Barbourofelis* had a short, sturdy skull with well-developed carnassial teeth but reduced chewing molars. The front of *Barbourofelis*'s lower jaw had vertical slots to accommodate the long, downward-curving upper canine teeth when the animal's mouth was closed.

Pachycrocuta (Middle Pleistocene, Eurasia and Africa). Modern hyenas are restricted to Africa and tropical India. Known for their tenacious bite, modern hyenas measure between 4 and 5 feet (1.2 and 1.5 m) long and weight up to about 125 pounds (55 kg). Their front legs are longer than their hind legs, and they are known as good runners that can stalk prey patiently for many miles without becoming exhausted. The earliest hyenas date from the Early Miocene; these animals were small, possibly insectivorous, civetlike animals such as *Ictitherium* (Late Miocene, Greece). The modern form of hyena, a creature that is both predator and scavenger, arose in the

Middle to Late Miocene and was widespread in Africa, Europe, and Asia.

Pachycrocuta was a more recent large form of hyena. Standing about 3.3 feet (1 m) tall at the shoulder, *Pachycrocuta* was about the size of a lion. This stocky beast probably was the largest of all hyenas. The lower limb elements were short, which made *Pachycrocuta* less of a runner and more of a powerful, short-range attacker. *Pachycrocuta* was a formidable animal. It probably competed ably with big cats for food and possibly stole their kills. *Pachycrocuta* became extinct following the last Ice Age, at about the same time as the saber-toothed cats. If indeed *Pachycrocuta* relied on scavenging kills made by saber-toothed cats, one can imagine that the demise of the big cats adversely affected the future of this giant hyena. Other, faster-moving taxa of hyenas survived, perhaps because they were better equipped to fend for themselves.

Ursus (Pleistocene to recent, Europe and Central Asia). *Ursus*, the Pleistocene cave bear, was an ancestor of modern grizzlies. The earliest bears date from the beginning of the Miocene. Even the earliest well-known bear taxa, such as *Agriotherium* (Late Miocene to Pleistocene, Africa, Asia, Europe), have generalized dentition that is best suited for a varied, omnivorous diet. This means that these carnivores already had developed a diet that was not limited to meat. These early bears also were more long-legged and taller than *Ursus*. Widespread during the last Ice Age, *Ursus* was an impressive omnivore with powerful jaws and large, flat cheek teeth for grinding tough vegetation or bones. Literally tens of thousands of individual cave bear specimens have been found in European caves; it is presumed that these large bears gathered in the caves during the harsh Ice Age winters. The skull of *Ursus* was massive and tall; some exceeded 20 inches (51 cm) in length. *Ursus* coexisted with early humans and was hunted by Neandertals.

Enaliarctos (Early Miocene, Western North America). Pinnipeds ("fin footed") include seals, sea lions, and walrus. Pinnipeds are true carnivores adapted for an aquatic life. An early stage in the adaptation of these animals from a terrestrial lifestyle to that of the water is seen in *Enaliarctos*, a 7-foot (2 m) swimming mammal found in California fossil beds. The robust limbs of *Enaliarctos* were much like those of its terrestrial ancestors, the bears, and it used both its fore- and hind limbs to propel itself through the water. Its hind limbs still were long and muscular and not reduced, as are the tiny hind limbs of modern sea lions. This indicates that *Enaliarctos* continued to spend much of its time on land. Other adaptations point more directly to sea lions. These adaptations include *Enaliarctos*'s large eyes; its lessened sense of smell, as indicated by a reduction in the olfactory bulbs of the brain; its improved hearing; and a modified nasal cavity that enabled *Enaliarctos* to hold its breath longer than its wholly terrestrial ancestors. *Enaliarctos* was about 5 feet (1.5 m) long.

Smilodon (Late Pleistocene, North and South America). *Smilodon* ("saber tooth") is the best-known saber-toothed cat. It is known from an abundance of specimens from North and South America. Three species of *Smilodon* are recognized; the largest was from South America and was as big as a lion. *Smilodon* had a strong, muscular body and a short tail. It was one of the most recently extinct of the saber-toothed cats, having died out about 10,000 years ago. Remains of more than 1,200 individuals of *Smilodon* have been recovered from the fossil tar pits of Rancho La Brea in California; this makes this extinct cat one of the best represented in the fossil record. The saber teeth of these cats were only partially exposed; they were rooted firmly in the upper part of the skull, on either side of the nostrils. In the largest species of *Smilodon*, the saber teeth could be as long as 11 inches (28 cm). A little more than half of that length was exposed and drooped below the chin when the mouth was closed. The skull mechanics of *Smilodon* allowed it to open its jaws up to 120 degrees. This enormous gape attests to *Smilodon*'s use of its saber teeth to stab a prey animal or rip a sizeable strip of flesh from its body.

The body plan of *Smilodon* was not quite like that of the modern, fleet-footed lion or tiger. Its forelimbs were stronger and more robust than its hind limbs. This suggests that it was more adept at attacking large, slow-moving animals with the brute strength of

Smilodon (Late Pleistocene, North and South America)

its upper body and jaws than it was at chasing and dragging down faster-running prey. *Smilodon*'s saber teeth were essentially banana shaped, somewhat flattened laterally, and serrated on both the leading and inside edges, much like a two-sided steak knife. The South American species of *Smilodon*, found in Argentina, evidently migrated there from the north when the two American continents became joined about 3.5 million years ago.

SUMMARY

This chapter explored the evolution and lifestyles of two important groups of predatory mammals, the Creodonta and the Carnivora.

1. The Creodonta and Carnivora were dominant Cenozoic predators with roots in the Early Paleocene. Both groups were descendants of a common ancestor, probably a group of insect eaters that dated back to the Late Cretaceous.
2. The extinct Creodonta lived from the Paleocene to the late Miocene and were the dominant carnivorous mammals of North America, Afric, Europe, and Asia during the early Cenozoic.

3. The creodont jaw had cutting cheek teeth set far back in the jaw. This made it more difficult for creodonts to consume anything but meat. True carnivores were more highly adapted to omnivory and a variety of food sources, which improved their fitness for survival.

4. Two subgroups of creodonts are known. The Oxyaenidae included catlike and bearlike forms. The Hyaenodontids included saber-toothed, doglike, and hyenalike forms.

5. The Carnivora are known for having a pair of carnassial, or meat-shearing, teeth, one on each side of the jaw.

6. Carnivora can be divided into three main groups: the Feliformes (cats, civets, and hyenas); the Caniformes (dogs, weasels, and bears); and an aquatic subgroup of the bears known as the Pinnipedia (seals, sea lions, and walrus).

7. Saber-tooth dentition is not unique to a single group of true carnivores; it has evolved independently several times in the evolution of mammals.

8

A DIVERSITY OF MAMMALS: GLYPTODONTS, SLOTHS, AND OTHER EUTHERIANS

The rise and eventual conquest of the mammals was slow in developing, even by geologic standards. After first appearing in the Late Triassic Epoch, more than 200 million years ago, small, insect-eating mammals lived their lives unobtrusively in the shadows of the dinosaurs. Only by the end of the Mesozoic Era, with the extinction of dinosaurs at hand, did mammals begin to develop larger body sizes and, in some habitats, effectively begin to compete with their dinosaurian neighbors. By the turn of the Cenozoic Era, 65 million years ago, the ancestral stock of eutherian and marsupial mammals was in place, poised to advance. As climates changed and the dinosaurs disappeared, these smart, highly adaptable, warm-blooded creatures persevered into available ecological niches.

Previous chapters in *The Age of Mammals* have explored major radiations of mammals that were most closely associated with the ascendancy of mammals over the planet: the radiation of marsupials of all forms, mostly to the southern continents; the rise of primates; the conquering of woodlands and grasslands by the remarkably diverse hoofed mammals; the rise of the spectacular elephants; and the radiation of sophisticated predatory mammals that rapidly evolved in size and diversity.

This chapter rounds out the story of mammalian evolution by examining several remaining and equally curious groups. These include the insectivores, descendants of the earliest mammals

(Insectivora); the rodents and rabbits (Glires); the pangolins (Pholidota); and the armadillos, sloths, and anteaters (Xenarthra). All of these mammal groups have living members; together, they serve as a dynamic testament to the fact that evolution can indeed favor some of the most peculiar and different kinds of organisms.

INSECTIVORA

True insectivores are a clan of small mammals that live a somewhat hidden and secretive existence and that are mostly active only at night. The modern groups of Insectivora include moles, shrews, and hedgehogs. It is assumed that the extinct ancestors of today's insectivores probably lived on diets as varied as those of their descendants, ranging from insects to worms, mollusks, and even tiny fish.

Insectivores have small bodies and burn calories quickly. This makes it necessary for them to spend the bulk of their waking hours in search of food. Many insectivores have adapted a tooth design that features triangular-shaped upper molars with a central, penetrating cusp for crushing the hard shells of prey. Other features shared by insectivores include complete mammalian dentition, five toes on each plantigrade foot, and a narrow skull with a small brain. As such, the insectivore body plan has changed little since the animals' emergence as the first true placental mammals in the Cretaceous **Period**, 85 million years ago.

Leptictidium (Middle Eocene, Europe). The small *Leptictidium* ("delicate weasel") was an early insectivore that resembled a long-snouted shrew with slender hind legs. The animal is known from excellent specimens found in the finely grained shale deposits of Messel, Germany. There, even the animal's stomach contents have been preserved. *Leptictidium* measured about 35 inches (90 cm) long, including its lengthy, bare, ratlike tail. Its forelimbs were so short that this small creature must have been a bipedal runner. *Leptictidium* probably scampered about in pursuit of food while running in a bent-forward posture with its tail held out as a counterbalance. Its short forelimbs could have been used to hold its food, almost in the manner of a mouse holding a piece of cheese. Fossilized stomach contents show that *Leptictidium* fed on small lizards and mammals as well as on insects.

Deinogalerix (Late Miocene, Europe). Hedgehogs were not always the darling little fur balls known today. *Deinogalerix* ("terrible hedgehog") was an enormous ancestor of the hedgehog that measured three times the length of the most common extant species. At about 24 inches (61 cm) long, this big-headed, long-snouted, long-legged insectivore was the size of a small dog. It used its long battery of teeth to poke around underbrush, trees, and holes to find insects to consume. *Deinogalerix* had stiffened hair on its body rather than the modified bristles (hollow hairs) found in living hedgehogs.

GLIRES: RABBITS, BEAVERS, AND RODENTS

Large, open-rooted incisors are one of the traits shared by all members of the clade Glires, a grouping of rabbits, hares, beavers, rats, mice, and guinea pigs that also has been reinforced by molecular evidence. Rodents in particular are a highly successful clade, represented today by more than 1,800 species. This makes rats, mice, and their kin the most varied and perhaps most populous group of living mammals. The larger **clade** Glires includes the two subgroups Rodentia and Lagomorpha.

The earliest members of the Rodentia were more squirrel-like than ratlike. They first radiated in North America during the Late Paleocene. The rapid spread of the rodents was due in part to their apparently having displaced another early, widespread—but now extinct—mammal clan, the multituberculates. While the term *rodent* usually conjures up images of urban, suburban, and rural pests such as mice and rats, the marvelous diversity and success of this clan are made more evident when one considers the varied domains of its other members: Squirrels live in woodlands and make their nests in trees; beavers occupy waterways, building dams and lodges of mud and sticks; guinea pigs are indigenous to South America, where they live in the foothills of the Andes. The deep-rooted incisors of rodents grow continuously. This leads to the animals' relentless need to gnaw wood, nuts, seeds, and other hard materials. The mechanics of the rodent jaw also are unusual. The bottom jaw can be protruded while the animal is gnawing, and chewing action within the mouth moves from the back to the front. A study of rodent jaw musculature and tooth wear by biologists William P. Wall and Sherri J. Hayes of Georgia College showed that these mechanics give rodents a two-phase chewing cycle: an ingesting phase during which the gnawing incisors are aligned, and a grinding phase that lines up the molars for the grinding of ingested food.

The Lagomorpha include rabbits, hares, and pikas. These animals differ from rodents in that they have two pairs of chisel-like upper incisors instead of the rodents' one pair. Lagomorphs also differ in the mechanics of their jaws. Lagomorphs chew in a sideways fashion rather than from back to front as rodents do. Like rodents, rabbits have teeth that grow continuously. The lagomorph hind limb is long and is adapted for the springlike action of hopping. The earliest rabbits arose in Asia from the Late Paleocene to the Early Eocene and were some of the most successful early herbivorous mammals.

Ischyromys (Early Eocene, North America). One of the earliest known rodents is *Ischyromys*. It was described originally by pioneering American paleontologist Joseph Leidy in 1856, based on a skull and jaw fragments. It was an abundant animal in the Oligocene of North America and is known today from dozens of specimens. *Ischyromys* was especially squirrel-like. It measured about 2 feet (60 cm) long, with flexible limbs and five clawed digits on each foot. These characteristics made it a good tree climber. *Ischyromys* had not yet developed the specialized back-to-front chewing action of modern rodents. Because this indicates that in *Ischyromys,* chewing was more up and down in nature and centered on the cheek teeth, *Ischyromys* probably was not quite as good at gnawing as later rodents.

Palaeolagus (Oligocene, North America). *Palaeolagus* ("ancient hare") was an early rabbit and not too far removed in time from the earliest known lagomorph, *Eurymulus* (Late Paleocene, Mongolia). Yet *Palaeolagus* was already extremely modern and rabbitlike, with a short tail, long ears, and a jaw structure already adapted for the side-by-side style of chewing characteristic of living rabbits.

The hind limbs of *Palaeolagus* were not entirely well adapted for the extreme hopping gait seen in modern rabbits, however, so *Palaeolagus* marks a transitional phase in the evolution of lagomorph locomotion.

Castoroides (Pleistocene, North America). The line of rodents that includes modern beavers had its origins in the Early Oligocene. The earliest members were smaller than modern beavers and more terrestrial; they also were better adapted for burrowing in the ground than for gnawing down trees. Two early members were *Steneofiber* (Early Miocene, Europe) and its North American cousin *Palaeocastor* (Early Miocene, North America). *Palaeocastor* has been associated with curious, corkscrew-shaped fossilized burrows cut by the animal's large incisors. The walls of these burrows still show the marks of the teeth and occasionally include the remains of one of these prehistoric beavers. During their evolution, beavers became bigger and better adapted for living in the water as the only remaining beavers do today. *Castoroides* was the largest beaver ever; it was about 8 feet (2.5 m) long and weighed as much as a small bear at about 440 pounds (200 kg). *Castoroides* had robust, gnawing teeth; short legs; and webbed feet. It was well adapted for swimming and for felling trees.

PHOLIDOTANS: THE PANGOLINS

Pangolins, or scaly anteaters, are a unique group of mammals with only seven species that survive today, in tropical regions of Africa and Asia. Pangolins are known for having a body covering of overlapping scales, an elongated skull with a toothless jaw, a long tongue, and the ability to seal the eyes and ears completely from outside pests. These adaptations advertise the pangolin's dietary preference for live ants; it ingests these with its tongue by sticking its snout into active ant nests. Sealing its eyes and ears allows the animal to keep ants out as the pangolin goes about its business. The scaly anteater also has long claws on its feet for digging. Pangolins have a lifestyle similar to that of true anteaters, which are classified as xenarthrans.

The fossil record for pangolins extends back to the Middle Eocene of Germany. The best-known pangolin fossil taxa come from the shale beds of Messel, Germany, and include *Eomanis* and *Palaeanodon* (Eocene, North America and Europe). The oldest member of the pangolin group is *Eomanis,* which strongly suggests that pangolins originated in Europe and later dispersed into Asia and Africa. Preserved stomach contents for extinct pangolins have confirmed that they ate plants as well as ants.

Pangolins' lack of teeth often makes fossilization especially rare. Some specimens, such as *Cryptomanis,* are recognized based only on traits of other, more generalized body parts, such as limbs. This makes the identification of pangolin fossils a challenge for any paleontologist. *Cryptomanis* was recognized as a pangolin only in 2005, even though its fossils were found originally in 1928 by an expedition from the American Museum of Natural History. Because the fossil of *Cryptomanis* lacked a skull or teeth, for more than 75 years, it was thought to be that of a creodont.

Eomanis (Middle Eocene, Germany). *Eomanis* measured about 20 inches (50 cm) long. It had a scaly body and an elongated snout like modern pangolins, but its tail lacked scales. The robust limbs of *Eomanis* show that it was well adapted not only for digging, but also for tree climbing. Living pangolins such as Manis are capable of rolling themselves into a ball as a defensive mechanism. The skeleton of *Eomanis* was not quite as flexible, and the animal probably was incapable of this maneuver. Modern species also have a long, prehensile tail to help them in climbing; this feature was not present in *Eomanis.* Such differences aside, *Eomanis* greatly resembled its living descendants in almost every way.

XENARTHRANS: ARMADILLOS, SLOTHS, AND TRUE ANTEATERS

The living forms of Xenarthrans include only a few taxa of relatively small, unobtrusive but unusual creatures: the sloths of Central and South America; the armadillos of North, Central, and South America; and the anteaters of Mexico, Central America, and South

America. The name Xenarthran ("extraneous joints") refers to additional articulations on their vertebral column to accommodate their trunk and tail parts. Other traits shared by this group include large claws; a fusion of the hip to the tail; and reduced dentition that varies from a lack of incisors to a total lack of teeth (as seen in the anteaters). Some, but not all, taxa have bony ossicles on their skin or a flexible, bony shield that covers most of the body.

Ancestral xenarthrans originated in South America and radiated north by the time of the Miocene. Xenarthran remains are widespread in the Pleistocene of North America. Armadillos were one of the first of the group to evolve; their remains, in the form of fossilized scutes, have been found in Late Paleocene deposits. These animals evolved into larger and larger forms with extraordinary outer bony shields; they form a group known as the glyptodonts that is best known from the Pliocene and Pleistocene of the Americas. These herbivores had massive, bulky skulls equipped with a battery of closely spaced cheek teeth reminiscent of the duck-billed dinosaurs. They were well adapted for grazing on tough plains grasses.

The fossil record of sloths goes back to the Oligocene. They began as partly arboreal animals that led the way to several giant forms across the Americas. More than 60 extinct taxa of ground sloths have been identified. They range from animals the size of small dogs to giants such as *Nothrotheriops* (Pleistocene, North America); *Megalonyx* (Pleistocene, North America); and *Megatherium* (Pleistocene, South America). The last named, at about 20 feet (6 m) long, is the largest known sloth. While the large-bodied ground sloths achieved giant proportions, one lineage of smaller, tree-living taxa continued and is the only group of sloths still alive, although represented today by only five species.

Anteaters are not represented well by the fossil record. The best fossil of a possible early anteater is *Eurotamandua* (Middle Miocene, Europe). Because *Eurotamandua* is from Europe, however, and all other xenarthrans are from the New World of the Americas, it is unlikely that this enigmatic, anteaterlike creature was related to the true anteaters. In its resemblance to *Eomanis*, a pangolin found in

Glyptodon (Pliocene to Late Pleistocene, North and South America) attacked by wild dogs.

the same German fossil location, *Eurotamandua* appears to represent an example of convergent evolution. In body form, *Eurotamandua* was similar to *Eomanis* in many ways, but *Eurotamandua* lacked scales.

Glyptodon (Pliocene to Late Pleistocene, North and South America). *Glyptodon* and its South American relative *Doedicurus* (Pleistocene, South America) exemplify the extreme size and heavily armored body plan of the largest forms of these rotund armadillos. *Glyptodon* was covered by a thick armor shield that was made up of smaller, polygonal scutes composed of bone. Its head was topped by another bony plate, and its tail was plated with bony studs. The uppermost body shield was tall, round, and deep. This allowed the animal to crouch down and fully enclose its legs within the protective shell. The bony scutes were arranged in concentric rings not unlike the armor of modern armadillos. Each individual scute was about 1 inch (2.5 cm) thick, and the entire protective carapace was composed of as many as a thousand such plates.

Glyptodon stood about 5 feet (1.5 m) tall, was about 11 feet (3.3 m) long, and weighed about 2 tons (2.2 tonnes); in other words, it had the heft of a small car. To support its enormous weight, *Glyptodon* had robust limbs and an especially massive hip girdle that was fused in two places to the vertebrae of the back. Its skull was deep, with massive jaws and special bony attachments in the cheek area for the added muscles needed to help it grind the tough grasses of the dry Argentinean plains. The teeth of *Glyptodon* were nestled deep in the cheek area and formed an excellent grinding surface.

Glyptodonts became extinct about 10,000 years ago. It is believed that humans living at the same time occasionally may have used the armor shell of a dead glyptodont as a temporary shelter against bad weather.

Megatherium (Pliocene to Late Pleistocene, North and South America). Extinct ground sloths of various sizes have been found throughout the Americas. *Nothriotheriops* (Pliocene to Pleistocene, North America) is well known from the Rancho La Brea tar pit site in California. It measured about 5 feet (1.6 m) long. One of the larger North America sloth taxa was *Glossotherium* (Pliocene to Pleistocene, North America), which measured about 13 feet (4 m) long and had the characteristically large head and inward-turned long claws recognized in most ground sloths. The largest ground sloth of all was *Megatherium* (gigantic beast), a gentle giant from Patagonia and other parts of South America. Measuring up to 20 feet (6 m) long and weighing about 3 tons (3.3 tonnes), this enormous plant eater probably reared up on its strong hind legs and used its arms to tug at trees and bring leaves and branches to its mouth. *Megatherium* had powerful jaw muscles for chewing plants and massive limbs with long, curved claws. Its hind limbs were much shorter than its forelimbs, and the nature of its foot bones required the animal to

Hapalops (Oligocene, Argentina) was a small South American ground sloth.

walk on the outside edges of its feet while keeping its claws off the ground. It was undoubtedly a slow-moving animal. Some specimens of *Megatherium* have been found as far north as Texas.

SUMMARY

This chapter examined several groups of mammals: the insectivores; the rodents and rabbits; the pangolins; and the armadillos, sloths, and anteaters.

1. The modern groups of Insectivora include moles, shrews, and hedgehogs. The earliest insectivores were the first true placental mammals; they first appear in the fossil record about 85 million years ago, in the Cretaceous Period.

2. The Glires include two subgroups: Rodentia and Lagomorpha. Large, open-rooted incisor teeth are one of the traits shared by all members of this clade, which includes rabbits, hares, beavers, rats, mice, and guinea pigs.

3. Rodents are a highly successful clade represented today by more than 1,800 species—more than any other mammal group.

4. The earliest members of the Rodentia were squirrel-like; they radiated in North America during the Late Paleocene. The earliest rabbits arose in Asia from the Late Paleocene to the Early Eocene.

5. Pangolins, or scaly anteaters, are a unique group of mammals with only seven species surviving today in tropical regions of Africa and Asia. The fossil record for pangolins extends back to the Middle Eocene of Germany; the oldest member of the group is *Eomanis*.

6. The living forms of xenarthrans include the tree sloths and the true anteaters, all of which are from the Americas.

7. Ancestral xenarthrans originated in South America and radiated north by the time of the Miocene. Armadillos were the earliest xenarthrans; they first appeared in the Late Paleocene. The fossil record of sloths goes back to the Oligocene; sloths began as partly arboreal animals, and their lineage led to several giant forms across the Americas. The fossil record of anteaters is very poor.

8. Most xenarthrans were extinct by about 10,000 years ago.

CONCLUSION

ICE AGE SETBACKS AND OPPORTUNITIES

At the turn of the Cenozoic Era, about 65 million years ago, Earth was undergoing a dramatic transformation of habitats that evidently was good for mammals. Continents moved; climates became temperate, with flowering plants, woodlands, and grasses growing in abundance; and mammals stepped into ecological niches left vacant by the extinction of the dinosaurs. Every part of the planet—including those areas, such as Antarctica, that today are considered frozen wastelands—was home to a widening diversity of mammals. Insect-eater carryovers from the Mesozoic led to increasingly sophisticated herbivores and carnivores of all sizes. Adaptations of jaws, teeth, skulls, limbs, and other traits led to mammals that were better adapted for every mode of life: swinging through trees, burrowing in the sand, scurrying along the forest floor, galloping across the open plains, or diving in the ocean.

Worldwide mammal diversity reached an astounding peak by the Middle Miocene, about 15 million years ago. Despite their geographic isolation from one another, mammal fauna from the Northern and Southern Hemispheres evolved some remarkably similar convergences, including look-alike families of hoofed browsers, horses, and predatory mammals. By the close of the Miocene, shifting continents and changing geologic conditions began to moderate the once uniformly comfortable Earth to more starkly defined zones that ranged from midlatitude tropics to polar ice caps. As Earth cooled, the tropics shrank; so, too, did the diversity of species.

The Great Ice Age of the Pleistocene began about 2 million years ago and plunged the planet into alternating spans of icily cold and moderately warm periods. Many mammals adapted, but many did not. By about 12,000 years ago, as the Ice Age drew to a close, mammal extinctions were underway on all continents. Large mammals were especially hard hit. According to paleontologist Michael Benton (b. 1956), 73 percent—equating to 33 genera—of large North American mammals died out at that time. Those that died out included mammoths, mastodonts, tapirs, sloths, glyptodonts, camels, and horses. South America was equally hard hit: It lost about 80 percent of its large mammal fauna. The numbers show that, as in North America, large mammals suffered the biggest losses. Wiped out were entire populations of elephantiforms, ground sloths, horned browsers, ancestral rhinoceroses, and others. Mammals that survived the Ice Age included many that could reproduce rapidly; many of these were smaller-bodied animals. The ability to reproduce rapidly offered these mammals a way to hedge their bets during a time of harsh environmental conditions.

Two somewhat conflicting reasons are given for the widespread Ice Age extinctions. The first is that large mammals were not able to adapt quickly enough to the changes in climate and food supplies as the planet alternately cooled and warmed. Another point of view correlates the loss of large mammal species with the rise of humans; the suggestion is that humans hunted the large mammals into extinction. Although there is no convincing anthropological evidence for the overhunting of large prehistoric mammals, the timing of the radiation of early humans and the loss of large mammals is a tempting relationship to ponder. Scientists on both sides of the argument continue to compile evidence in support of one point of view or the other.

Primates and the stock from which human ancestors eventually arose were well established by the Miocene. The evolutionary stage was set for the development of one of the most peculiar mammal taxa of all: humans, who would emerge as the most dominant mammals of all time. The biology and evolution of the human species is the subject of two other books in this series, *Primates and Human Ancestors* and *Early Humans*.

APPENDIX ONE:
GEOLOGIC TIME SCALE

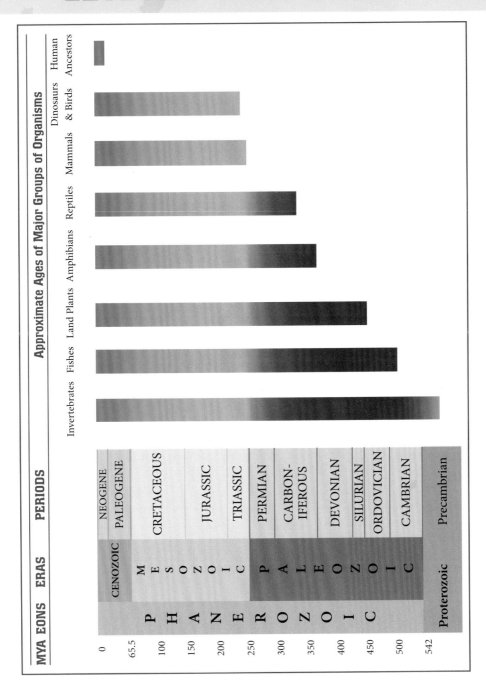

APPENDIX TWO: POSITIONAL TERMS

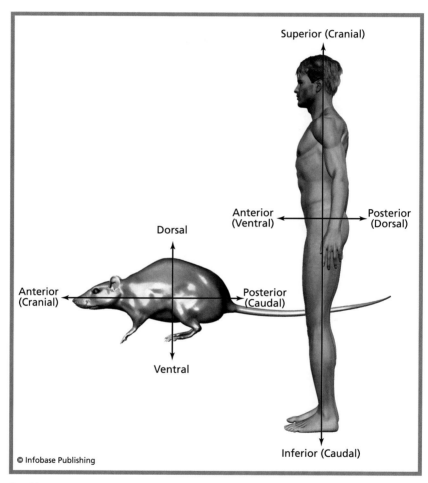

© Infobase Publishing

Positional terms used to describe vertebrate anatomy

GLOSSARY

adaptations   Anatomical, physiological, and behavioral changes that occur in an organism that enable it to survive environmental changes.

Ameridelphia   Marsupials of North and South America.

anatomy   The basic biological systems of an animal, such as the skeletal and muscular systems.

anterior   Directional term meaning toward the head, or cranial, end of a vertebrate.

anthropoids   Higher primates (monkeys, apes, and humans).

Artiodactyla   Subgroup of ungulates that includes the even-toed hoofed mammals.

articulated   Condition of a fossil skeleton found with its bones in place, connected as they would have been in life.

Australidelphia   Australian marsupials.

basal   At or near the base or earliest level of evolutionary development; a term usually used to refer to an ancestral taxon.

binocular vision   Overlapping vision of the two eyes.

bone bed   Fossil locality with a high concentration of bones from more than one individual.

brachiation   Swinging from branch to branch using grasping arms and legs.

Carnivora   Group of carnivorous mammals that includes cats, dogs, hyenas, bears, and seals.

carnivorous   Meat-eating.

Cetartiodactyla   Subgroup of ungulates that includes the whales and dolphins.

clade   A group of related organisms including all the descendants of a single common ancestor.

convergent evolution   Term used to describe a situation in which unrelated species each develop similar adaptations to similar environmental conditions.

Creodonta   Group of carnivorous mammals that lived from the Paleocene to the Miocene in North America, Africa, Europe, and Asia.

derived   Term used to describe a trait of an organism that is a departure from the most basal (ancestral) form.

digitigrade   Term used to describe vertebrates that walk on their toes.

era   A span of geologic time ranking below the eon; the Archean Eon is divided into four eras dating from more than 4 billion years ago to 2.5 billion years ago; the Proterozoic Eon is divided into three eras dating from 2.5 billion years ago to about 542 million years ago; the Phanerozoic Eon is divided into three eras, the Paleozoic, the Mesozoic, and the Cenozoic; the Paleozoic ("ancient life") Era lasted from 542 million to 251 million years ago; the Mesozoic ("middle life") Era lasted from 251 million to 65 million years ago; the Cenozoic ("recent life") Era began 65 million years ago and continues to the present.

euprimates   Basal (primitive) members of the primates.

eutherian   Mammal that gives birth to young after an extended gestation period during which the embryo is nourished by means of a placenta, a temporary organ found in females during pregnancy; also called a placental mammal.

evolution   The natural process by which species gradually change over time, controlled by changes to the genetic code—the DNA—of organisms and whether or not those changes enable an organism to survive in a given environment.

extant   Term used to describe an organism that is living today; not extinct.

extinction   The irreversible elimination of an entire species of organism because it cannot adapt effectively to changes in its environment.

fauna   Animals found in a given ecosystem.

flora   Plants found in a given ecosystem.

forelimbs   The two front legs of a vertebrate.

fossil   Any physical trace or remains of prehistoric life.

gene   A portion of a DNA strand that controls a particular inherited trait.

genus   (plural: genera) A taxonomic name entity for one or more closely related organisms that is divided into species; names of organisms, such as *Tyrannosaurus rex*, are composed of two parts, the genus name (first) and the species name (second).

geographic isolation   The isolation of species on a land formation as a result of naturally occurring geologic events (e.g., formation of an island or of mountains).

herbivore   An animal whose primary food source is vegetation.

heterodont   Having different kinds of teeth in different zones of the jaw.

hind limbs   The two rear legs of a vertebrate.

hominids   Fossil and living humans.

ice age   Periodic span of cooling that results in the development of ice sheets, or glaciers, that extend from the poles and lower global average temperatures.

interglacial period   A span of planet warming during an ice age.

K-T extinction   Mass extinction of the dinosaurs and other organisms that occurred at the boundary between the Late Cretaceous Epoch and the Tertiary/Paleocene Epoch.

lophodont   Word used to describe molar teeth with transverse ridges joining the cusps, thereby creating a more effective grinding surface; a mammal with such teeth.

mass extinction   An extinction event that kills off more than 25 percent of all species in a million years or less.

marsupial   Mammal whose young are born early, in a state that is little more than embryonic; once born, most marsupial offspring are suckled within the safety of a pouch.

natural selection   One of Darwin's observations regarding the way in which evolution works; given the complex and changing conditions under which life exists, those individuals with the combination of inherited traits best suited to a particular environment will survive and reproduce while others will not.

New World   The Americas.

Old World   Africa, Asia, and Europe.

olfactory   Related to the sense of smell.

omnivorous   Eating a diet consisting of both plants and meat.

Paenungulata   Mammal group that includes the elephants and their relatives.

paleontologist   Scientist who studies prehistoric life, usually using fossils.

Pangaea   Earth's major landmass that formed during the Permian and lasted until the end of the Triassic Period and that later broke apart into two smaller landmasses, Laurasia and Gondwana.

period   A span of geologic time ranking below the era; the Phanerozoic Eon is divided into three eras and 11 periods, each covering a span of millions of years; the longest of these periods, including the three in the Mesozoic Era, are further broken down into smaller divisions of time (epochs).

Perissodactyla   Subgroup of ungulates that includes odd-toed hoofed mammals.

placental mammal   Mammal that gives birth to young after an extended gestation period during which the embryo is nourished by means of a placenta, a temporary organ found in females during pregnancy; also called a eutherian.

plantigrade   Term used to describe vertebrates that walk flat-footed, with the soles of their feet on the ground.

population   Members of the same species that live in a particular area.

postcranial   "Behind the head"; term generally used to refer to the portion of the vertebrate skeleton other than the head.

posterior   Directional term meaning toward the tail end; also known as the caudal end.

predator   Animal that actively seeks, kills, and feeds on other animals.

prosimians   Lower primates (lemurs, lorises, and tarsiers).

ruminant   Grazing animal with multiple digestive chambers and the ability to rechew partially digested food that is returned to the mouth.

sedimentary   Term used to describe rock that forms in layers from the debris of other rocks or the remains of organisms.

sexual dimorphism   Variation in morphology between males and females of a species.

species   In classification, the most basic biological unit of living organisms; members of a species can interbreed and produce fertile offspring.

taxon   (plural: taxa) In classification, a group of related organisms, such as a clade, genus, or species.

trackway   Series of sequential animal footprints.

transitional   Representing one step in the many stages that exist as species evolve.

ungulate   Hoofed mammal.

CHAPTER BIBLIOGRAPHY

Preface

Wilford, John Noble "When No One Read, Who Started to Write?" *The New York Times* (April, 6, 1999). Available online. URL: http://query. nytimes.com/gst/fullpage.html?res=9B01EFD61139F935A35757C0A9 6F958260. Accessed March 31, 2008.

Chapter 1 – Extinct Marsupials of North and South America

Eberle, Jaelyn, and John E. Storer. "Herpetotherium Valens (Lambe), A Didelphid Marsupial from the Calf Creek Local Fauna (Chadronian), Saskatchewan." *Journal of Vertebrate Paleontology* 15, No. 4 (1995): 785–794.

Flannery, T.F. "New Pleistocene Marsupials (Macropodidae, Diprotodontidae) from Subalpine Habitats in Irian Jaya." *Alcherringa* 16 (1992): 321–331.

Goin, Francisco J., Judd A. Case, Michael O. Woodburne, Sergio F. Vizcaíno, and Marcelo A. Reguero. "New Discoveries of Opposum-like Marsupials from Antarctica (Seymour Island, Medial Eocene)." *Journal of Mammalian Evolution* 6, No.4 (December 1999): 335–365.

Kemp, T.S. *The Origin and Evolution of Mammals.* Oxford: Oxford University Press, 2005.

Kurtén, Björn. *The Age of Mammals.* New York: Columbia University Press, 1971.

Martin, James E., Judd A. Case, John W.M. Jagt, Anne S. Schulp, and Eric W.A. Mulder. "A New European Marsupial Indicates a Late Cretaceous High-Latitude Transatlantic Dispersal Route." *Journal of Mammalian Evolution* 12, Nos. 3–4 (December 2005): 495–511.

Pascual, Rosendo, Francisco J. Goin, and Alfredo A. Carlini, "New Data on the Groeberiidae: Unique Late Eocene-Early Oligocene South American Marsupials." *Journal of Vertebrate Paleontology* 14, No. 2 (1994): 247–259.

Pickrell, John. "Oldest Marsupial Fossil Found in China." *National Geographic News* (December 15, 2003). Available online. URL: http://news.nationalgeographic.com/news/2003/12/1215_031215_oldestmarsupial.html. Accessed March 31, 2008.

Prothero, Donald R. *After the Dinosaurs: The Age of Mammals.* Bloomington: Indiana University Press, 2006.

Raven, Peter H., George B. Johnson, Jonathan B. Losos, and Susan R. Singer. *Biology,* 7th ed. New York: McGraw-Hill, 2005.

Rothecker, J., and John E. Storer. "The Marsupials of the Lac Pelletier Lower Fauna, Middle Eocene (Duchesnean) of Saskatchewan. *Journal of Vertebrate Paleontology* 16, No. 4 (1996): 770–774.

Savage, R.J.G. *Mammal Evolution: An Illustrated Guide.* New York: Facts on File, 1986.

Chapter 2 – Extinct Marsupials of Australia

Anderson, C. "Fossil Marsupials from New Guinea." *Palaeontological Notes No. 4; Records of the Australian Museum* 20 (1937): 73–76.

Archer, Michael, Suzanne Hand, and Henk Godthelp. "A New Order of Tertiary Zalambdodont Marsupials." *Science* 239, No. 4847 (March 25, 1988): 1528–1531.

Benton, Michael. *Vertebrate Paleontology,* 3rd ed. Oxford: Blackwell Publishing, 2005.

Bown, T.M., and E.L. Simons. "First Record of Marsupials (Metatheria: Polyprotodonta) from the Oligocene in Africa." *Nature* 308 (March 29, 1984): 447–449.

Kemp, T.S. *The Origin and Evolution of Mammals.* Oxford: Oxford University Press, 2005.

Kurtén, Björn. *The Age of Mammals.* New York: Columbia University Press, 1971.

Menzies, J. "An Early Date for a Diprotodon (Marsupialia; Diprotodontidae) from the Papua New Guinea Highlands." The Australian and Pacific Science Foundation. Available online. URL: http://www.apscience.org.au/projects/PBF_01_9/pbf_01_9.htm. Accessed March 31, 2008.

Muirhead, Jeanette. "*Yaraloidea* (Marsupialia, Peramelemorphia), A New Superfamily of Marsupial and a Description and Analysis of the Cranium of the Miocene Yarala Burchfieldi." *Journal of Paleontology* 74, No. 3 (May 2000): 512–523.

Prothero, Donald R. *After the Dinosaurs: The Age of Mammals.* Bloomington: Indiana University Press, 2006.

Raven, Peter H., George B. Johnson, Jonathan B. Losos, and Susan R. Singer. *Biology,* 7th ed. New York: McGraw-Hill, 2005.

Savage, R.J.G. *Mammal Evolution: An Illustrated Guide.* New York: Facts on File, 1986.

Chapter 3 – Last of the Archaic Eutherians

Adkins, R.M., and R.L. Honeycutt. "Molecular Phylogeny of the Superorder Archonta." *Proceedings of the National Academy of Sciences* 88 (1991): 10317–10321.

Beard, K. Christopher. "Searching for Our Primate Ancestors in China." Carnegie Museum. Available online. URL: http://www.carnegiemuseums.org/cmag/bk_issue/1996/marapr/beard.htm Accessed March 31, 2008.

———. "Gliding Behaviour and Palaeoecology of the Alleged Primate Family Paromomyidae (Mammalia, Dermoptera)." *Nature* 345, (May 24, 1990): 340–341.

Beard, K. Christopher, Leonard Krishtalka, and Richard K. Stucky. "First Skulls of the Early Eocene primate Shoshonius cooperi and the Anthropoid-Tarsier Dichotomy." *Nature* 349 (January 3, 1991): 64–67.

Benton, Michael. *Vertebrate Paleontology,* 3rd ed. Oxford: Blackwell Publishing, 2005.

Bloch J.I., and M.T. Silcox. "Cranial Anatomy of the Paleocene Plesiadapiform Carpolestes simpsoni (Mammalia, Primates) Using Ultra High-Resolution X-ray Computed Tomography, and the Relationships of Plesiadapiforms to Euprimates." *Journal of Human Evolution* 50, No. 1 (2006): 1–35.

Bloch, Jonathan I., and Doug M. Boyer. "Grasping Primate Origins." *Science* 298, No. 5598 (November 22, 2002): 1606–1610.

Bloch, Jonathan I., Mary T. Silcox, Doug M. Boyer, and Eric J. Sargis. "New Paleocene Skeletons and the Relationship of Plesiadapiforms to Crown-Clade Primates." *Proceedings of the National Academy of Sciences* 104, No. 4 (Janaury 23, 2007): 1159–1164.

Kemp, T.S. *The Origin and Evolution of Mammals.* Oxford: Oxford University Press, 2005.

Kurtén, Björn. The Age of Mammals. New York: Columbia University Press, 1971.

Prothero, Donald R. *After the Dinosaurs: The Age of Mammals.* Bloomington: Indiana University Press, 2006.

Savage, R.J.G. *Mammal Evolution: An Illustrated Guide.* New York: Facts on File, 1986.

Chapter 4 – The Archonta: Tree Shrews, Flying Lemurs, Bats, and Primates

Adkins, R.M., and R.L. Honeycutt. "Molecular Phylogeny of the Superorder Archonta." *Proceedings of the National Academy of Sciences* 88 (1991): 10317–10321.

Beard, K. Christopher. "Searching for Our Primate Ancestors in China." Carnegie Museum. Available online. URL: http://www.carnegiemuseums.org/cmag/bk_issue/1996/marapr/beard.htm. Accessed March 31, 2008.

———. "Gliding Behaviour and Palaeoecology of the Alleged Primate Family Paromomyidae (Mammalia, Dermoptera)." *Nature* 345, (May 24 1990): 340–341.

Beard, K. Christopher, Leonard Krishtalka, and Richard K. Stucky. "First Skulls of the Early Eocene primate Shoshonius cooperi and the Anthropoid-Tarsier Dichotomy." *Nature* 349 (January 3, 1991): 64–67.

Benton, Michael. *Vertebrate Paleontology*, 3rd ed. Oxford: Blackwell Publishing, 2005.

Bloch, Jonathan I., Doug M. Boyer. "Grasping Primate Origins." *Science* 298, No. 5598 (November 22, 2002): 1606–1610.

Bloch, Jonathan I., Mary T. Silcox, Doug M. Boyer, and Eric J. Sargis. "New Paleocene Skeletons and the Relationship of Plesiadapiforms to Crown-Clade Primates." *Proceedings of the National Academy of Sciences.* 104, No. 4 (Janaury 23, 2007): 1159–1164.

Chopra, S.R.K., and Vasishat, R.N. "Sivalik Fossil Tree Shrew from Haritalyangar, India." *Nature* 281, No. 5728, (1979): 214–215.

Hartwig, Walter Carl, and Castor Cartelle. "A Complete Skeleton of the Giant South American Primate Protopithecus." *Nature* 381 (May 23, 1996): 307–311.

Kemp, T.S. *The Origin and Evolution of Mammals.* Oxford: Oxford University Press, 2005.

Kurtén, Björn. *The Age of Mammals.* New York: Columbia University Press, 1971.

Prothero, Donald R. *After the Dinosaurs: The Age of Mammals.* Bloomington: Indiana University Press, 2006.

Rafferty, Katherine L., Alan Walker, Christopher B. Ruff, Michael D. Rose, and Peter J. Andrews. "Postcranial Estimates of Body Weight in Proconsul, with a Note on a Distal Tibia of *P. major* from Napak, Uganda." *American Journal of Physical Anthropology* 97, No. 4 (April 27, 2005): 391–402.

Raven, Peter H., George B. Johnson, Jonathan B. Losos, and Susan R. Singer. *Biology,* 7th ed. New York: McGraw-Hill, 2005.

Savage, R.J.G. *Mammal Evolution: An Illustrated Guide.* New York: Facts on File, 1986.

ScienceDaily. "Giant Ape Lived Alongside Humans." (November 13, 2005) Available online. URL: http://www.sciencedaily.com/releases/2005/11/051112122318.htm Accessed March 31, 2008.

Wallace, David Rains. *Beasts of Eden.* Berkeley: University of California Press, 2004.

Wong, Kate. "Shaking the Family Tree: A New Fossil Leaves Former Theories Out on a Limb." *Scientific American* (January 26, 1998). Available online. URL: http://www.sciam.com/article.cfm?id=000BC5A8–4B81–1CE0–B4A8809EC588EEDF&ref=sciam. Accessed March 31, 2008.

Chapter 5 – Hoofed Mammals: The Ungulata

Bajpai, Sunil, and Philip D. Gingerich. "A new Eocene Archaeocete (Mammalia, Cetacea) from India and the Time of Origin of Whales." *Evolution* 95, No. 26 (December 22, 1998): 15464–15468.

Benton, Michael. *Vertebrate Paleontology,* 3rd ed. Oxford: Blackwell Publishing, 2005.

Bramble, D.M. "Origin of the Mammalian Feeding Complex: Models and Mechanisms." *Paleobiology* 4, No. 3 (1978): 271–301.

Eisenberg, J.F. *The Mammalian Radiations: An Analysis of Trends in Evolution, Adaptation, and Behavior.* Chicago: University of Chicago Press, 1981.

Gingerich, Philip D. "Land-to-Sea Transition in Early Whales: Evolution of Eocene Archaeoceti (Cetacea) in Relation to Skeletal Proportions and Locomotion of Living Semiaquatic Mammals." *Paleobiology* 29, No. 3 (September 2003): 429–454.

Kemp, T.S. *The Origin and Evolution of Mammals.* Oxford: Oxford University Press, 2005.

Kurtén, Björn. *The Age of Mammals.* New York: Columbia University Press, 1971.

Menzies, J.I., and C. Ballard. "Some New Records of Pleistocene Megafauna from New Guinea." *Science in New Guinea* 20 (1994): 113–139.

Prothero, Donald R. *After the Dinosaurs: The Age of Mammals.* Bloomington: Indiana University Press, 2006.

Raven, Peter H., George B. Johnson, Jonathan B. Losos, and Susan R. Singer. *Biology,* 7th ed. New York: McGraw-Hill, 2005.

Savage, R.J.G. *Mammal Evolution: An Illustrated Guide.* New York: Facts on File, 1986.

Turner, Alan. *Evolving Eden.* New York: Columbia University Press, 2004.

Wallace, David Rains. *Beasts of Eden.* Berkeley: University of California Press, 2004.

Chapter 6 – Mammoths, Elephants, and Their Relatives: The Paenungulata

Bramble, D.M. "Origin of the Mammalian Feeding Complex: Models and Mechanisms." *Paleobiology* 4, No. 3 (1978): 271–301.

Butler, P.M. "Some Functional Aspects of Molar Evolution." *Evolution* 26, No. 3 (1972): 474–483.

Eisenberg, J.F. *The Mammalian Radiations: An Analysis of Trends in Evolution, Adaptation, and Behavior.* Chicago: University of Chicago Press, 1981.

Kemp, T.S. *The Origin and Evolution of Mammals.* Oxford: Oxford University Press, 2005.

Kurtén, Björn. *The Age of Mammals.* New York: Columbia University Press, 1971.

Prothero, Donald R. *After the Dinosaurs: The Age of Mammals.* Bloomington: Indiana University Press, 2006.

Raven, Peter H., George B. Johnson, Jonathan B. Losos, and Susan R. Singer. *Biology,* 7th ed. New York: McGraw-Hill, 2005.

Savage, R.J.G. *Mammal Evolution: An Illustrated Guide.* New York: Facts on File, 1986.

Turner, Alan. *Evolving Eden.* New York: Columbia University Press, 2004.

Wallace, David Rains. *Beasts of Eden*. Berkeley: University of California Press, 2004.

Chapter 7 – Big Cats, Hyenas, Dogs, Bears, and Their Relatives: The Carnivores and Creodonts

Bramble, D.M. "Origin of the Mammalian Feeding Complex: Models and Mechanisms." *Paleobiology* 4, No. 3 (1978): 271–301.

Eisenberg, J.F. *The Mammalian Radiations: An Analysis of Trends in Evolution, Adaptation, and Behavior*. Chicago: University of Chicago Press 1981.

Kemp, T.S. *The Origin and Evolution of Mammals*. Oxford: Oxford University Press, 2005.

Kurtén, Björn. *The Age of Mammals*. New York: Columbia University Press, 1971.

Prothero, Donald R. *After the Dinosaurs: The Age of Mammals*. Bloomington: Indiana University Press, 2006.

Raven, Peter H., George B. Johnson, Jonathan B. Losos, and Susan R. Singer. *Biology*, 7th ed. New York: McGraw-Hill, 2005.

Savage, R.J.G. *Mammal Evolution: An Illustrated Guide*. New York: Facts on File, 1986.

Turner, Alan. *Evolving Eden*. New York: Columbia University Press, 2004.

———. *The Big Cats and Their Fossil Relatives*. New York: Columbia University Press, 1997.

Wallace, David Rains. *Beasts of Eden*. Berkeley: University of California Press, 2004.

Wroe, Stephen, Colin McHenry, and Jeffrey Thomason. "Bite Club: Comparative Bite Force in Big Biting Mammals and the Prediction of Predatory Behaviour in Fossil Taxa." *Proceedings of the Royal Society B: Biological Sciences* 272, No. 1563 (March 22, 2005): 619–625.

Chapter 8 – A Diversity of Mammals: Glyptodonts, Sloths, and Other Eutherians

Benton, Michael. *Vertebrate Paleontology*, 3rd ed. Oxford: Blackwell Publishing, 2005.

Kemp, T.S. *The Origin and Evolution of Mammals*. Oxford: Oxford University Press, 2005.

Kurtén, Björn. *The Age of Mammals*. New York: Columbia University Press, 1971.

Prothero, Donald R. *After the Dinosaurs: The Age of Mammals.*
  Bloomington: Indiana University Press, 2006.

Raven, Peter H., George B. Johnson, Jonathan B. Losos, and Susan R.
  Singer. *Biology,* 7th ed. New York: McGraw-Hill, 2005.

Savage, R.J.G. *Mammal Evolution: An Illustrated Guide.* New York: Facts
  on File, 1986.

Turner, Alan. *Evolving Eden.* New York: Columbia University Press, 2004.

Wall, William, and Sherri J. Hayes. "A Biomechanical Analysis of
  Mastication in the Fossil Rodent *Ischyromys* and its Bearing on
  the Origin of Sciuromorphs." Department of Biology, Georgia
  College. Available online. URL: http://www.nature.nps.gov/geology/
  paleontology/pub/grd2/gsa04.htm. Accessed March 31, 2008.

Wallace, David Rains. *Beasts of Eden.* Berkeley: University of California
  Press, 2004.

FURTHER READING

Agusti, Jordi, and Mauricio Anton. *Mammoths, Sabertooths, and Hominids*. New York: Columbia University Press, 2002.

Benton, Michael. *Vertebrate Paleontology*, 3rd ed. Oxford: Blackwell Publishing, 2005.

Colbert, Edwin H., and Michael Morales. *Evolution of the Vertebrates*, 4th ed. New York: Wiley-LSS, 1991.

Ellis, Richard. *No Turning Back: The Life and Death of Animal Species.* New York: HarperCollins, 2004.

Kemp, T.S. *The Origin and Evolution of Mammals*. Oxford: Oxford University Press, 2005.

Lucas, Spencer G. *Chinese Fossil Vertebrates*. New York: Columbia University Press, 2001.

Margulis, Lynn, and Karlene V. Schwartz. *Five Kingdoms: An Illustrated Guide to the Phyla of Life on Earth*, 3rd ed. New York: W.H. Freeman, 1998.

Norman, David. *Prehistoric Life: The Rise of the Vertebrates*. New York: Macmillan, 1994.

Palmer, Douglas. *Atlas of the Prehistoric World*. New York: Discovery Books, 1999.

Prothero, Donald R. *After the Dinosaurs: The Age of Mammals.* Bloomington: Indiana University Press, 2006.

Raven, Peter H., George B. Johnson, Jonathan B. Losos, and Susan R. Singer. *Biology,* 7th ed. New York: McGraw-Hill, 2005.

Savage, R.J.G. *Mammal Evolution: An Illustrated Guide*. New York: Facts on File, 1986.

Stock, Chester. *Rancho La Brea: A Record of Pleistocene Life in California*, 6th ed. Los Angeles: Los Angeles County Museum of Natural History, 1968.

Turner, Alan. *The Big Cats and Their Fossil Relatives*. New York: Columbia University Press, 1997.

———. *Prehistoric Mammals*. Washington, D.C.: National Geographic Society, 2004.

Turner, Alan, and Mauricio Anton. *Evolving Eden*. New York: Columbia
University Press, 2004.

Wallace, D.R. *Beasts of Eden*. Berkeley: University of California Press,
2004.

Web Sites

American Museum of Natural History. Vertebrate Evolution

An interactive diagram of vertebrate evolution with links to
example fossil specimens in the world-famous collection of this
museum.

**http://www.amnh.org/exhibitions/permanent/fossilhalls/
vertebrate/**

Australian Museum. Palaeontology

An extensive visual guide to Australian fossils.

http://www.austmus.gov.au/palaeontology/index.htm.

Clowes, Chris. Paleontology Page

A privately compiled but exhaustive resource on many paleontology
subjects, including a valuable look at the Burgess Shale fossils.

http://www.peripatus.gen.nz/Paleontology/Index.html

International Commission on Stratigraphy. International Stratigraphic Chart

Downloadable geologic time scales provided by the International
Commission on Stratigraphy.

http://www.stratigraphy.org/cheu.pdf

Lapworth Museum, University of Birmingham. Palaeontological Collections: Vertebrate Collection

Online exhibit exploring early vertebrate life from the United
Kingdom.

**http://www.lapworth.bham.ac.uk/collections/palaeontology/
vertebrates.htm**

Kazlev, Alan, and Augustus White. Palaeos: The Trace of Life on Earth

A robust and growing reference about all kinds of life-forms.

http://www.palaeos.com/

Maddison, D.R., and K.-S. Schulz. The Tree of Life Web Project

The Tree of Life Web Project is a meticulously designed view of life-forms based on their phylogenetic (evolutionary) connections. It is hosted by the University of Arizona College of Agriculture and Life Sciences and the University of Arizona Library.

http://tolweb.org/tree/phylogeny.html

Paleontology Portal. Vertebrates

A resource exploring early vertebrate life, produced by the University of California Museum of Paleontology, the Paleontological Society, the Society of Vertebrate Paleontology, and the United States Geological Survey.

http://www.paleoportal.org/index.php?globalnav=fossil_ gallery&sectionnav=taxon&taxon_id=16

Public Broadcasting Service. Evolution Library: Evidence for Evolution

This resource outlines the extensive evidence in support of both the fact and theory of evolution, basing its approach on studies of the fossil record, molecular sequences, and comparative anatomy.

http://www.pbs.org/wgbh/evolution/library/04/

Scotese, Christopher R. Paleomap Project

A valuable source of continental maps showing the positioning of Earth's continents over the course of geologic time.

http://www.scotese.com/

University of California Museum of Paleontology. Fossil Evidence: Transitional Forms

A tutorial about transitional forms in the fossil record, with illustrated examples.

http://evolution.berkeley.edu/evosite/lines/IAtransitional.shtml.

Virtual Fossil Museum. Fossils Across Geological Time and Evolution

A privately funded, image-rich educational resource dedicated to fossils. Contributors include amateur and professional paleontologists.

http://www.fossilmuseum.net/index.htm

Picture Credits

Page

23: © Infobase Publishing
24: © Infobase Publishing
25: © Infobase Publishing
27: © Larry Miller/Photo
    Researchers, Inc.
27: © Infobase Publishing
39: © Michael Long/NHMPL
41: © Infobase Publishing
42: © Irina Yun/iStockphoto
44: © Infobase Publishing
45: © De Agostini/NHMPL
47: © Michael Long/NHMPL
53: © Infobase Publishing
57: Artwork © Mauricio Anton
58: © Michael Long/NHMPL

75: Artwork © Mauricio Anton
81: © Infobase Publishing
82: © Infobase Publishing
85: © Mark A. Klingler/
    Carnegie Museum of
    Natural History
99: Artwork © Mauricio Anton
118: John Sibbick
119: John Sibbick
125: Getty Images
130: John Sibbick
145: John Sibbick
152: Artwork © Mauricio Anton
161: John Sibbick
163: John Sibbick

INDEX

About the Author

THOM HOLMES is a writer specializing in natural history subjects and dinosaurs. He is noted for his expertise on the early history of dinosaur science in America. He was the publications director of *The Dinosaur Society* for six years (1991–1997) and the editor of its newsletter, *Dino Times*, the world's only monthly publication devoted to news about dinosaur discoveries. It was through the Society and his work with the Academy of Natural Sciences in Philadelphia that Thom developed widespread contacts and working relationships with paleontologists and paleo-artists throughout the world.

Thom's published works include *Fossil Feud: The Rivalry of America's First Dinosaur Hunters* (Silver Burdett Press, September, 1997); *The Dinosaur Library* (Enslow, 2001–2002); *Duel of the Dinosaur Hunters* (Pearson Education, 2002); *Fossil Feud: The First American Dinosaur Hunters* (Silver Burdett/Julian Messner, 1997). His many honors and awards include the National Science Teachers Association's *Outstanding Science Book of 1998*, VOYA's 1997 Nonfiction Honor List, an Orbis Pictus Honor, and the Chicago Public Library Association's *"Best of the Best"* in science books for young people.

Thom did undergraduate work in geology and studied paleontology through his role as a staff educator with the Academy of Natural Sciences in Philadelphia. He is a regular participant in field exploration, with two recent expeditions to Patagonia in association with Canadian, American, and Argentinian universities.